What people are saying about ..

Singing in Babylon

"Impactful and timely, this book will help us navigate the new terrain we find ourselves in, and remind us that we are here for such a time, for such a place as this."

Mark Batterson, author and lead pastor
of National Community Church

"Practical, inspirational, and full of hope."

Sorted Magazine

"Jeff understands and dispenses grace with passion, humor, and thoughtful content—a rare combination."

Philip Yancey, award-winning author

"My long-time friend Jeff Lucas is one of the most original thinkers I know and is one of the most interesting writers of our time. I wish I could write like he does! And speak like he does! His treatment of Daniel will grip you from start to finish."

Dr. R. T. Kendall, teacher, speaker, and
author of more than fifty books

"This is such an important message for all those of us who sometimes fear that life is passing us by, that God's best lies elsewhere, and that the pain in our past must inevitably diminish our destiny. It's also an important message for 'now'—for the deeply troubled times in which we live. Jeff Lucas is a trusted guide whose insights have influenced my life for decades, always with honesty, good humor, and relentless grace."

Pete Greig, 24-7 Prayer International
and Emmaus Rd church, UK

"Pastor Jeff continues to deliver fresh and life-giving content to the church. This is a necessary and inspired book. Read, reflect on, and live this message. It's time … let the volume of the music rise and the new lyrics be heard—it's time to sing again."

Daniel Rolfe, senior pastor of Mountain
Springs Church, Colorado Springs

"Jeff Lucas's book on Daniel is a refreshing, vibrant, and challenging look at life in a 'second choice' world.… It's a prophetic word for our times and I couldn't recommend it more highly."

Paul Reid, pastor emeritus of Christian
Fellowship Church, Belfast, Northern Ireland

"With powerful, practical, and amazingly pertinent insights, Jeff has written a book that imparts God's wisdom to us, especially during this coronavirus crisis."

Lyndon Bowring, chairman of CARE

"A time of pandemic: dreams put on hold, illness and death overtaking our friends and family, shut in, human contact curtailed.

Where's God in all this? … God's there in the mess—and the God who held Daniel and his friends in exile holds us and the church today. This is a book for our times—for this strangest time."

Pete Broadbent, bishop of Willesden

"Jeff has this incredible way of touching the depth of our hearts with honesty, humor, and clear-sighted wisdom. I can't commend this book to you enough."

Carl Beech, president of CVM
(Christian Vision for Men)

"In *Singing in Babylon*, Jeff doesn't offer platitudes. *He tells us a story.…* He reminds us that, even when life doesn't hand us our first choice, God will take us by the hand and bring meaning from our mess. No one tells a Bible story like Jeff Lucas, and this book just proves that point!"

Troy Champ, lead pastor of Capital Church,
Salt Lake City and Park City, Utah

"One of the many things that I've come to appreciate about Jeff is the way that he combines a deep love for the Scriptures with a pastoral care for the people he's ministering to. This book is no exception. Here, Jeff expertly unpacks the ancient story of Daniel in a way that can significantly impact our lives today. Read and be encouraged!"

Dave Smith, senior pastor of Kingsgate
Community Church, Peterborough

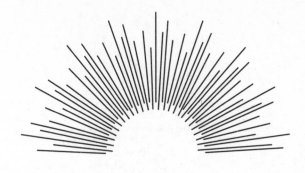

SINGING
in
BABYLON

FINDING PURPOSE
IN LIFE'S
SECOND CHOICES

JEFF LUCAS

transforming lives together

SINGING IN BABYLON
Published by David C Cook
4050 Lee Vance Drive
Colorado Springs, CO 80918 U.S.A.

Integrity Music Limited, a Division of David C Cook
Brighton, East Sussex BN1 2RE, England

The graphic circle C logo is a registered trademark of David C Cook.

The website addresses recommended throughout this book are offered as a
resource to you. These websites are not intended in any way to be or imply an
endorsement on the part of David C Cook, nor do we vouch for their content.

Unless otherwise noted, all Scripture quotations are taken from THE HOLY
BIBLE, NEW INTERNATIONAL VERSION®, NIV® Copyright © 1973, 1978,
1984, 2011 by Biblica, Inc.® Used by permission. All rights reserved worldwide.
Scripture quotations marked THE MESSAGE are taken from THE MESSAGE. Copyright
© by Eugene H. Peterson 1993, 2002. Used by permission of Tyndale House
Publishers, Inc. The author has added italics to Scripture quotations for emphasis.

Library of Congress Control Number 2020942649
ISBN 978-0-8307-7871-3
eISBN 978-0-8307-8147-8

© 2021 Jeff Lucas International Ministries

The Team: Ian Matthews, Ali Hull, Megan Stengel, Susan Murdock
Cover Design: James Hershberger
Cover Image: Getty Images

Printed in the United States of America
First Edition 2021

1 2 3 4 5 6 7 8 9 10

111820

Contents

To Kay, who has lived with me through
the writing of thirty books.
Kay's preference would have been to stay at home,
but we've trekked millions of miles together.
I'm forever grateful.

Acknowledgments

First and foremost, I'm most grateful to Viv Thomas. In his wonderful book, *Second Choice: Embracing Life as It Is*, he introduced me to the language of "second choice" life. I have quoted him extensively, and I'm thankful for his permission to utilize his brilliance in the formation of this book.[1]

My thanks also to Gerard Kelly, a wonderful poet and wordsmith. We worked together for years in the leadership of Spring Harvest, and Gerard's study guide, *Sing the Lord's Song in a Strange Land*, created for the Spring Harvest event back in 2005, has been an invaluable resource.[2]

My thanks to Ian Matthews and the team at David C Cook, and to my brilliant editor for decades now, Ali Hull.

Prelude

It was a poignant moment, and the room hushed as if to mark it.

Huddled around a lengthy conference table for our weekly pastors meeting, we chattered back and forth, considering themes for an upcoming sermon series. Someone posed a question.

"What are we hearing from people in our congregation?"

There was a thoughtful pause, then Pastor Brent spoke up:

"There's one comment I hear repeatedly, expressed in a variety of ways. People often say that life just hasn't turned out the way they thought it would."

A senior member of our team, sage-like Dick Foth, smiled ruefully and nodded. He's navigated quite a few twists in the road during his seventy-something trips around the sun.

"Life is what happens when you expected something else," he mused.

Through a window across the room, beams of sunshine cascaded through the glass, the cloudless sky a shimmering blue.

We were in Fort Collins, Colorado. Boasting around three hundred days of sunshine annually, our city often scores top marks in those "Best places to live" charts. Fort Collins is seen as an ideal location for raising a family, with quality schools and the prestigious Colorado State University nestled in the historic down-town area, which also hosts a thriving arts scene and more than fifteen microbreweries.

This northern Colorado city is viewed as a great place to retire, affordable, with a multitude of restaurants that appeal to every taste. There are well-stocked libraries and lush parks and great health care.

The population is broadly affluent. As in any city, some face economic hardship, but the median family income tops $90,000.

The Front Range of the majestic Rocky Mountains dominates the horizon to the west. People hike, camp, hunt, jog, and ski, in an outdoorsy, healthy culture.

It's not perfect, but it is very pleasant.

Yet it was here people were reporting that life just hadn't turned out the way they thought it would. And the comment was coming, not from those who had yet to discover the power and purpose that Jesus offers, disappointed because life without God seemed hollow. This was a view from Christians who were wrestling with "second choice" life.

As we'll see (and I'll emphasize this repeatedly), life for every one of us, Christians included, involves episodes or seasons that would not be our first choice. We all live on a fractured planet, cre-ated good but now marred by the Fall, where everything is not as it should be. Thus in the trivial and the tragic, life can be good, but it's rarely perfect, if ever.

So how can we find purpose when the sun disappears from view and all seems barren, wintry?

That's what this book is about. We will spend time with a man who was suddenly wrenched from a life of privilege and roughly shoved into an existence of servility and danger. His was not a brief visit; we will see that he would spend his whole life in that second choice world, but he did not merely survive in that place: he flourished. Many miles from family and home, he surely experienced great heartache, but he also discovered that God had trekked to Babylon with him. I will not visit every detail that Scripture gives us about Daniel. The first six chapters of the book that bears his name focus on stories about Daniel and his friends, and the second six chapters focus on prophetic material about the future. We will focus more on the stories than the prophecies. I want to highlight enough of his journey to illustrate this truth:

In the midst of bewildering dislocation, Daniel found that his God helped, delivered, spoke, directed.

The result?

In short, in Babylon, Daniel sang.

Perhaps, where you live, life just hasn't turned out the way you thought it would.

My prayer is that, in these pages, you and I might find grace, hope, and purpose as we follow Daniel's footsteps and, more specifically, consider Daniel's God.

I have a request. Please don't be tempted to gloss over or ignore the portions of Scripture that will follow: they come from God's Word and provide vital context for all I have written.

Thank you for allowing me to journey with you in this book. Together, may we learn how to hum a tune when life happens, and we expected something else.

In the third year of the reign of Jehoiakim king of
Judah, Nebuchadnezzar king of Babylon came to
Jerusalem and besieged it. And the Lord delivered
Jehoiakim king of Judah into his hand, along with
some of the articles from the temple of God. These
he carried off to the temple of his god in Babylonia
and put in the treasure house of his god.

Daniel 1:1–2

How can we sing the songs of the
LORD while in a foreign land?

Psalm 137:4

To God's elect, exiles scattered …

1 Peter 1:1

Anyone who loves me will obey my teaching.
My Father will love them, and we will come
to them and make our home with them.

John 14:23

Now faith is confidence in what we hope for and assurance
about what we do not see. This is what the ancients
were commended for … who through faith … shut the
mouths of lions [and] quenched the fury of the flames.

Hebrews 11:1–2, 33–34

1

You've Been Relocated

I'm dreaming.

I'm a contestant in one of those so-called reality TV shows. My fellow cast members and I have been dropped into a hostile jungle location, where an alarmingly hungry number of creepy-crawlies vie for the epicurean opportunity to snack on humans.

It's a competition, and there's a handsome prize for the most enduring soul in the group.

It's my dream and I'll win if I want to.

I do.

I brave the slithery horrors of the snake pit. I wolf down a surprisingly crunchy maggot tart, and I am now declared winner.

My prize? My wife, Kay, and I can now relocate to anywhere we want to live in the world, the first year there all expenses paid. Our choice.

My first choice would be Hawaii, one the most remote groups of islands in the world, around 2,500 miles from the nearest continental landmass.

Thanks to frequent flier miles, I've been there a few times, and I love it.

Warm, soft, white sand underfoot, crystal clear blue water lapping at your toes as you stroll down the beach for your morning cappuccino.

Glorious sunsets where, like a laughing, slightly crazy artist, God lobs buckets filled with hundreds of shades of orange and red all over the fading blue canvas of sky, and the distant sun seems to settle, sizzling, into the sea.

The fresh after-rain aroma of the flora-perfumed air.

A gentle evening breeze that refreshes and never chills.

First choice. It doesn't get any better than this.

But stop right there. It seems that paradise is flawed.

There have been issues with rumbling volcanic activity, and not just the "vog" that can shroud the sun and stain the air with the rotten egg stench of sulphur dioxide, a toxic gas. Running from a fast-moving stream of bubbling molten lava (1,200 degrees hot) would not be my first choice.

Last time I was in Hawaii, I viewed a surfboard, structurally revised by a passing peckish shark that took a huge bite out of it. No harm was done to the surfer, but the beaches were closed for two days. Suddenly I can hear that menacing theme music from the movie *Jaws*.

Okay, perhaps it's unlikely that I'd bump into a hungry shark or suffer cremation courtesy of an angry volcano.

But there are other challenges. Living in such a remote place sounds idyllic, but being far from the madding crowd also means living distant from family and friends. One could easily be lonely in paradise.

Then there are those pesky tourists, lots of them. I've been one of them, but as a newly settled resident, I'd bristle when they crowd and litter the beach, grab the last table at the cafe, and purloin "my" parking space.

I know, these are very much first-world problems, the minor pains of the privileged few. For significant second choice challenges, I could have pointed to the millions who don't have enough food to feed their children today.

My point is this: even when life looks close to perfect, it's not. Real life is a combination of first and second choices. Every day includes some of both.

And, to emphasize the point, that is true for all who live on this beautiful yet broken planet, including those who follow the King whose rule is breaking in, but is not fully here yet. That Second Coming day will dawn, but in the meantime, we all have to live through mean and menial times.

We'd do well to face the truth, that in the trivial and the tragic, the irritating and the devastating, second choices—circumstances that we would not choose, given the chance—are part of living. But that reality check is often hindered by the way some portray the life of faith.

The preacher was working up a sweat now, dark patches appearing in the armpits of his otherwise immaculate suit. Arms flailing, he paced back and forth across the platform, barking into the microphone. His sky-blue eyes were wide open, his smile broad, revealing perfect white teeth.

What he offered sounded very good indeed. Bible open in hand, he proffered what everyone with a pulse wants: a wonderful life.

Briskly weaving contemporary examples of victory and break-through with a practiced delivery of memorized Scriptures, he told us that God wanted us—each and every one of us—to be winners, not losers.

We were to be the head, not the tail.

Triumphant over the circumstances, not cowed down by them.

Strong and healthy, not withered by sickness.

Financially prosperous, never short of cash.

Yes, please, I thought.

For a few moments, I believed it and tried to ignore the fact he had wrenched some of those Scriptures completely out of context. His rapid-fire, staccato delivery made it hard to keep up.

But my discomfort increased as I looked around the congregation. Like hungry baby sparrows, beaks wide open for a tasty tidbit, many of them were swallowing this whole.

Yes, please!

But then I glanced over at wheelchair-bound Sue, and before I could look away, she caught my eye. She just looked back at me, a fixed stare, yet not harsh. And then I realized what was behind her expression: quiet despair.

Her look seemed to probe me for some kind of silent response to the performance on the platform. Would I shrug, roll my eyes, shake my head? It felt as though she was alone, marooned, and now some gesture from me might lessen her stricken isolation.

Sue's condition has gone downhill fast in recent years. She has received prayer for her multiple sclerosis many times, but without noticeable effect. Once, another enthusiastic visiting evangelist loudly declared her healed and attempted, without success, to persuade her to vacate her wheelchair. She tried so hard to oblige, but couldn't even stand up straight, never mind take a step. She slumped back down heavily into the chair, a picture of defeat. The evangelist had no problem with his walking, darting to the next person in the queue for prayer.

Unwilling to commit to a gesture of response to Sue, I wondered if I was being wise or cowardly. I looked away, and my eyes fell upon Bill, who has been unemployed for a very long time. After decades of working for the same company (and refusing lucrative offers along the way because he is loyal), now he's been rudely banished in the company reshuffle, with the news he's now overqualified. He's too old, it seems; younger blood is needed. He lives daily with the harsh knowledge he has passed his sell-by date. His loyalty wasn't reciprocated.

Sitting next to him is his best friend, John, who is currently at the head of the proverbial tale, at least in career terms. Handsome and brilliant, he is racing through promotions at meteoric speed. With no money problems, he and his wife, Christine, enjoy the comforts of a beautiful home.

At first glance, they're living the dream. But John and Christine are currently navigating heartbreak because their oldest son has marched away from Jesus and is playing fast and loose with hard drugs. They pray for him each night before they vainly pursue sleep, terrified at the thought of a phone call in the small hours from the hospital or police.

Then I look across at the gaggle of smiling teenagers sitting cross-legged close to the platform; minutes ago they were bopping away as the worship band strutted their stuff. They recently completed high school, and the guest speaker at their graduating ceremony told them they could do anything they dreamed; if they believed it, it could be done. Now they were getting the "Christian" version of the same speech from our guest speaker.

It was then that I wondered: Were we setting these young people up with the expectation they would always experience a first choice world?

Where, if they put God first, they would get a life of comfort and abundance?

Where opportunity would knock but tragedy not stop by?

Where the sun would warm their backs but never burn their skin?

Bluntly, to do so is to indoctrinate them with a lie. Little wonder some struggle—and tragically, some even opt out of life—when it doesn't work out that way.

Nobody gets a life of endless first choices, be they billionaires or barely scraping by, be they anonymous faces in the crowd or feted celebrities.

Nobody.

Including Jesus.

If in doubt, eavesdrop on His prayers in Gethsemane. His first choice was for the cup of suffering to be taken away. He got second choice, which involved a cross.

Second choice living: we all experience it.

If in doubt, ask Sue.

Ask Bill.

Ask John and Christine.

Ask Jesus.

But here is some good news. When life offers us second choice, not only can we survive, we can thrive. We can flourish when the weather turns wintry.

I know those last couple of sentences sound like fodder churned out by one of those motivational speakers that I mentioned earlier, slogan-like rather than substantial. But as one who views the Bible as the core foundation for life, I'm convinced there's good reason for that claim.

Can we learn to blossom in the wilderness or, to switch back to our familiar metaphor, could we sing a joyful song in Babylon?

Perhaps there's a way.

Yes, please.

Here's another dream, more a nightmare.

You are living happily in the location of your choice. Life is good, comfortable, happily predictable.

War suddenly breaks out, and a totally unexpected defeat comes at the hands of a foreign power. Ground troops invade the country that you thought was yours, swooping across the land like ravenous locusts. Terror grips you as you watch the doom-laden newsflashes, because the headlines are apocalyptic. Rumors abound about the brutality of the advancing soldiers, who are rapidly approaching your area.

The dreaded day dawns. Enemy soldiers arrive, and pound on the door. They order you to pack your things: your home no longer belongs to you. Not that you will be homeless. It looks worse than that, because you are being deported, shipped off to that foreign country, together with some other leaders and influencers from the community. All your plans, hopes, dreams—your whole life—all has been snatched from your grasp.

Choices? You have none right now, and the horizon looks bleak.

At last you arrive in the place where you will be forced to settle and make your home, but it is an alien place, where everything is unfamiliar. Again, you have no choice. Nobody is asking what you think, if you like it here. You're a commodity. You've been trafficked.

You wonder: Where is God in all of this? Is He there? Worse still, if He is there, does He care?

As we turn to the story of Daniel, which unfolded 2,600 years ago, around 600 years before Christ, we see he faced an unexpected development that he would never have chosen: and one he would live with for the rest of his days. Deported, probably as a hostage, with a few friends to the strange land of Babylon, he was now in a location and situation where absolutely everything about the culture—music, food, customs, religion, philosophy, education, values—was all utterly foreign to him. Daniel, a contemporary of the fiery prophet Ezekiel, was a young man whose name means "God is my judge." Now he was suddenly caught up in the maelstrom in what was an extended period of exile, the judgment of God upon His wayward people.

Countless Sunday school teachers have portrayed Daniel as the suave hero in a real-life thriller story, but that depiction is wrong. Daniel's story is one of long-term captivity and conflict. As Larry Osbourne writes:

> It's such a huge mistake to turn Daniel into an
> adventure story. It not only obscures the main

point, but it also sends a blatantly false message:
if we do the right thing, God won't let anything
bad happen to us. He'll rescue us from the furnace
and the lions. Yet nothing could be further from
the truth. God's best have often suffered the worst
this world has to offer. Ever since the fall of Adam
and Eve, evil and injustice have had a field day. Bad
things happen to good and godly people all the
time.[3]

In Babylon, Daniel and his friends were a long way from the
comforts and familiarity of home. They were young, described in
the story as *yeladim*, a Hebrew word that was frequently used for
"lads." Some commentators say they may have been between twelve
and, at the most, eighteen. Historians believe that Babylonian
children began serious education at the age of fourteen, and that
Nebuchadnezzar would have demanded impressionable youngsters
who could be shaped by a rigorous training program. The Hebrew
boys were certainly inexperienced with life and therefore pliable.

Or so it was thought.

They had also lost particular privileges that were theirs back in
Jerusalem. Scripture tells us those chosen for service in the foreign
palace were from "the royal family and the nobility" (Dan. 1:3).
Rabbinic tradition says that Daniel was a descendant from King
Hezekiah—but now he was placed in someone else's service.

Ironically, if Daniel was indeed from the line of Hezekiah, then
his personal captivity and exile had been predicted by Isaiah around
150 years earlier:

"And some of your descendants, your own flesh and blood who will be born to you, will be taken away, and they will become eunuchs in the palace of the King of Babylon" (Isa. 39:7).

The mention of eunuchs brings us to another uncomfortable truth not usually mentioned in those Sunday school lessons.

Commentators are divided, but it's possible that hope for a normal marriage and family life was taken from the exiles shortly after they arrived at their new address: these young men were castrated. Hardly anyone's first choice, and devastating because in the ancient world the ability to have a family was especially vital. They were the ones who would not only inherit your wealth, but take care of you in your dotage. If you had no sons, you would lose your land to others. You would be forgotten.

There's no mention of any family in the story of Daniel and his friends, which is telling. And then he was "qualified" to work in the king's palace, which included a harem full of beautiful women. We know from the biblical record that Daniel was good-looking: a first choice. But that may have been the reason for an awful second choice: castration to appease the despot on the throne and protect his interests.

Daniel's "tutor" in the palace had already experienced the unkindest cut: according to the ESV translation of the text, he was the "chief of the eunuchs." Perhaps Daniel was part of an emasculated team, one that nobody would choose to join.

In the story of Daniel, Babylon is not just a location, but it represents a whole system of opposing beliefs and values: the city of this world against the city of God, a conflict traced in Scripture from Genesis to Revelation. Daniel's story poses the question: Who is the biggest loser? Daniel, beaten hands down by the power of Babylon, or God, vanquished by Babylon's gods? In those days, when a nation was defeated, people considered that the nation's God was defeated too.

Gerard Kelly comments:

> The taking of the secured articles from the temple in Jerusalem indicates that this is a spiritual as well as a political victory. There is a conflict between Babylon and Israel in which Israel is the loser. But behind this there is an implied conflict between the gods of Babylon and Israel's God, Yahweh. One of the primary questions the book of Daniel wrestles with is this: "Is it that Israel has lost power, or the God of Israel?" On the surface, we wonder if Daniel can survive the experience of exile, but far more deeply the book is asking us if Yahweh can survive it. Is God's "turf" limited to the promised land or will He still be God when all appears lost?[4]

Babylon personified evil.

The king whom they were forced to serve, Nebuchadnezzar, was impulsive, murderous, and vicious beyond belief, and his plundering of the temple was a deliberate act of mockery and blasphemy. This was a man who built a ninety-foot statue of himself and insisted that everyone bow before it.

Exile was devastating, separating these young men from all that they held precious.

They left behind the Promised Land—the place of God's bountiful provision, and the temple—viewed by the Jewish people as the place where God dwelled on the earth.

They were separated now from the holy and beloved city of Jerusalem, so cherished in the history of God's people, together with the comforting and strengthening cycles of sacrifice, celebration, feast, and festival, where God's people gathered to celebrate their unity and identity, and to renew their covenant with the Lord.

The city of Babylon itself would have been intimidating. The Babylonians were enjoying stunning economic and military success, having decisively triumphed over the armies of Assyria and Egypt in the battle of Carchemish.

Babylon was a boomtown.

Archeologists and Greek historians describe a fabulous and opulent designer city, built on both sides of the river Euphrates: the greatest and largest city on earth at that time. Two hundred miles square, it was surrounded by a double fortified wall, with 250 towers placed at strategic intervals. The walls, fifty-six miles of them, were eighty feet thick and 320 feet high.

The city was dominated by the Etemenanki: the temple of "the foundation of heaven and earth," a seven-story ziggurat dedicated to Marduk. At around 299 feet high, it was a skyscraper of its day, a staggering feat of engineering.

Parks, fields, and gardens took over 90 percent of the city, with the remainder filled with private houses, public buildings, and temples: over a thousand of them. Idolatry was everywhere. There was a huge double gate created to honor the god Ishtar, which led to a processional street especially designed for pomp and ceremony, decorated with enamel figures of dragons and bulls.

The hanging gardens, one of the Seven Wonders of the Ancient World, were situated in Nebuchadnezzar's palace.

The Babylonians had the wealth, the power, the architectural brilliance. The Hebrew Four had been taught that the idols of other nations were nothing, dead, powerless. But if that was true, how come they had all this "blessing"?

Even though the king was the most powerful man on earth, the belief was that the gods were the real power brokers. In Babylon, the temple priests wielded enormous power.

John Lennox says of them, "They controlled a great deal of the land and therefore were in receipt of immense revenues. Even the emperor had to publicly acknowledge that reality. At the climax of the spring festival Nebuchadnezzar had to submit to a public ritual humiliation by the priests, during which the custom was to slap him hard until his tears flowed. This was to remind everyone that the priests were the power behind the throne, and it was only after this ceremony had been performed that the great banquet to herald the advent of spring could begin."[5]

The land around the city was flat and fertile, in marked contrast to the land back in Judah. The plenty of Babylon mocked the lack of their homeland. Historians say that even the geography of Babylon daily reminded the exiles of what they'd lost. Babylon was quite literally a strange land, so unlike the mountains of Judah. The Judeans were hill-dwellers; historians say that being forcibly transported to a land of unending plains would have been bewildering. It was coupled with the sense that they'd been betrayed by their leaders and abandoned by God, intensifying their sense of emotional and spiritual crisis.

The plains offered nowhere to hide, no way to escape.

While they knew this had happened as a result of God's judgment, they must have wondered: *Why now? Why us?*

Why me? What did I do?

Not everything has a cause and effect. When things go wrong in life, it's not correct to suggest this is always the result of something bad we've done. But in Israel's case, exile came because she had consistently defied the Lord.

God had warned His people that persistence in evil would lead to captivity:

"You will be uprooted from the land you are entering to possess. Then the LORD will scatter you among all nations, from one end of the earth to the other" (Deut. 28:63–64).

So for hundreds of years warnings had been sounded. Gerard Kelly points out:

> The people of Israel should not have been surprised
> by the exile—there are plenty of hints in their earlier

history that such a thing could happen, and that dis-
obedience could trigger it. But for the most part they
did not read these signs and it was the trauma of
exile that finally convinced them that God was serious in both the promises and sanctions of covenant.
The prophets had spoken of it already but it took the
harsh reality of Babylon to bring the message home.[6]

Exile came because Israel refused to learn her lesson; judgment
came to bring her to her senses, calling her to repent from her idolatry
and its twin sister, injustice. And Daniel and his friends were caught
up in the maelstrom that resulted.

Mother sobbing, wailing. Begging
the soldiers to have mercy.
Take whatever you want, she screams, but please!
Leave my son!
One of them punches her hard in the face.
She falls heavily, and then a sword
is held at her throat.
Get in line, the man with the sword yells
at me, his filthy, yellow teeth gritted.
Do as you're told, or she dies.
Hands at her face, blood running through her
fingers, her sobs quieten now, but her body heaves.

I get in line, and there is one of them at my side,
almost willing me to make a wrong move.
I dare not look back.
What will become of us?
Will they march us out of the city,
and then put us to the sword?
Will there be torture first, with me
begging like my mother, not to be spared
but allowed the mercy of death?
The word is these invaders like to put out the
eyes of their enemies before they kill them.
A fool asks one of them: What will you do with us?
The others are coming with us to the
great city, Babylon, one of them says.
There's a long march ahead. Four
months. A dangerous route.
Babylon? A city of darkness.
What is there for us?
Prison?
A public execution, after a parade for the
victorious, with us as the trophies of war?
The fool pushes his luck.
What do you mean, the others
are going to Babylon?
It is the last thing he says.

So what's all this got to do with us, thousands of years later?

We've been relocated. We too live in exile.

It's always true of Christians that we live as foreigners, exiles, resident aliens. Exile is the place where we are not fully at home yet, and where God is not fully in charge—yet.

And that is where we live.

One day every knee will bow, but for now, the world remains broken. We are establishing a kingdom colony as we live as the people of God, and one bright day the new Jerusalem will come down, and the good King will fully take charge. In the meantime, we are resident aliens, living here but with a passport from another kingdom. As Gerard Kelly says,

> The New Testament points us to the truth that we Christians are "aliens and strangers" (Heb. 11:13; 1 Pet. 1:1; 2:11) living freely in the world and yet not at home within it. The Greek words used in these texts present a local church as a colony of resident aliens in a given place and time. We are called to be both resident and alien, at home but not at home in every place to which the spirit of God scatters us.[7]

And surely we feel that sense of alienation increasingly as the days go by.

Without developing an over-rosy view of a past where Christianity and churchgoing were more central in life, we must face the fact that culture has increasingly shifted away from

Christian values. Those who hold those values are often viewed as being out of touch and dismissed as intolerant, judgmental, even dangerous.

We are in exile, which is where the church began. In fact, they were an exilic people among an exiled people. Birthed in a nation that was governed by the occupying Roman forces (and therefore, in a sense, exiled within their own nation), they were initially a tiny minority, viewed as a strange sect within Judaism.

Again we must abandon the myth that following Jesus always give us a "first choice" life, and expose the fantasies associated with that myth.

As Viv Thomas suggests, there are four main fantasies:

> Fantasy one: "If I walk closely with God he will give me my first choice." The idea behind this fantasy is simple; it is the notion that spiritual people always "get it right." They listen to God and God always delivers to them the things they think they need. Really spiritual people are like high-class machinery—low maintenance and almost problem-free. If they do have problems they know how to solve them quickly.

> Fantasy two: "In my first choice world I will be happy." In this fantasy my peace and joy are dependent on getting my first choice. If I get what

I want I will be truly happy and content. Anything which appears to me to be second best will not do, for it will not give me the joy I think I need, and will thus make it impossible for me to live my life as I think I should be able to live it.

Fantasy three: "In my first choice world I will be secure." If I get what I want I will be able to build my life involving minimal risk. The underlying idea is that I do really know what is best for me so that I can actually make sure that I live a life which is long, safe, satisfied and under my control. In this fantasy second choice worlds are perceived as risky, difficult, undesirable and unstable.

Fantasy four: "In my first choice world I will be able to walk closely with God." This fantasy promises that when I am where I want to be then I will be able to have a wonderful relationship with God. When I get my first choice world it will help me understand his beauty, wonder and glory.[8]

A poignant example of "second choice living" comes from the experience of getting older and frailer, from writer Donald McCullough:

Every other week I visit a friend who lives in a convalescent home. I have a vague discomfort … I think I know what causes it: the fear of losing control. Examples of how this could happen abound in a convalescent home. Some residents are unable to leave the premises without assistance from relatives or friends; some are confined to wheelchairs; some need others to translate their incoherent mutterings; I don't like being reminded of the possibility of these things. Each loss, no matter how apparently small, is a blow to our freedom.[9]

Exile was not all bad news. In Daniel's case, it was God who "handed Israel over" to bring them to repentance and a greater revelation of His character. Exile was not just about judgment, but a tool to bring Israel clarity that might lead to a better day. Babylon was a place of revelation for Daniel.

God wanted His people to learn some lessons: walking away from Him had consequences. Ultimately, He is sovereign and in control. The place of suffering can be the place of refinement and growth. The darkest place can be the valley where we find light, and become the light to others. The hottest furnace can produce the purest gold.

Exile gave Daniel an unparalleled opportunity to speak into the dark realm of Babylonian politics.

Anyone who says that Christians should not be engaged in politics has never read or understood the book of Daniel. He speaks the truth of God to kings, and remember, he does this as a foreigner in exile. Up until now prophets of Israel have spoken to the kings of Israel, but this was a new situation. Exile has made Daniel and his friends aware that the God of Israel is the God of all creation, of all history, and of all peoples, everywhere.

Although these truths about God being the Lord of the planet and not just Israel were embedded in the call of Abraham and the commissioning of Moses, they come fully to the forefront in Daniel's exile.

And the book of Daniel has much more to show us about God too. In fact, that's the main purpose of the book. Although the story of Daniel is about ethics, it's not really a call to copy Daniel: to choose vegetarianism or open our windows to pray three times a day. It is not just a call to heroism. Like the book of Jonah, where too much focus has been given to the big fish, but which is primarily about God and His nature, the book of Daniel is really about Daniel's God.

As Tremper Longman points out, from its very first verses, the book of Daniel is not about Daniel but about God, who "does not reveal Himself to us in the abstract but rather in relationship to His people and through His actions in history."[10]

The revelation of God in the book of Daniel challenges many modern notions we have about God.

Daniel's God is mighty, and towers above the self-promotion yet undeniable power of King Nebuchadnezzar. God is totally self-sufficient, omniscient, and omnipotent. He is willing to share secrets about current and future events. He is far above anything humanity is or could ever hope to be; he is King of Kings, Lord of Lords, who does that which is humanly impossible. God acts, Nebuchadnezzar's jaw drops, and on one occasion, he falls prostrate because of what God does.

Daniel's God stands astride history, using it, never dominated or surprised by it. In spite of present appearances, He is in control. We don't live in a world where God's will is always done—that's why we pray, "Your kingdom come, Your will be done," but like the book of Revelation, the book of Daniel shows us that, ultimately, He is in charge, and finally, when Christ comes, He will rule and reign absolutely.

Even in chaos, God has a plan and a purpose. He works with the found and seeks the lost.

Perhaps most of all, Daniel's God was with him, wherever they found themselves, regardless of their circumstances.

Jesus knows about exile. In a sense, the incarnation of Jesus—His coming to this earth—was an experience of *total* exile, as He laid aside His majesty and the glories of heaven, exchanging them for the challenges and difficulties of life on this planet. As a baby, He was taken to a foreign land, Egypt, to escape Herod's program of infanticide. He experienced rejection from His own village, Nazareth, and had to relocate His base to Capernaum. As I mentioned earlier, in Gethsemane, He asked the Father if there was any other way to complete His work other than taking the pathway to the cross, a request that was denied, and so He experienced the ultimate "second choice"—a death sentence from Pilate. Jesus knows all about exile, and is able to fully empathize with us in our experience of exile and second choice living.

"For we do not have a high priest who is unable to empathize with our weaknesses, but we have one who has been tempted in every way, just as we are—yet he did not sin. Let us then approach God's throne of grace with confidence, so that we may receive mercy and find grace to help us in our time of need" (Heb. 4:15–16).

We live in Babylon.

But just as Daniel and his friends discovered that God lived where they lived too, so we affirm that God has taken up residence with us, in us, and will work through us, even as we live in a strange land. Jesus promised His followers pressure and presence. While we are never assured that we will not go through the fire, we are always assured that, in the agony of the fire, we are not and will never be abandoned. Wherever we find ourselves, and whatever circumstances are ours, we share our address with Him.

FOR REFLECTION

1. "Poor choices sometimes lead to second choice lives." What are some examples of this, and are there any from your own experience?

2. As Christians living in the Western Hemisphere, do you agree that we are now in exile? Why, or why not?

3. Can you give any example where you learned something valuable in a "second choice" circumstance—what was it?

Then the king ordered Ashpenaz, chief of his court officials, to bring into the king's service some of the Israelites from the royal family and the nobility—young men without any physical defect, handsome, showing aptitude for every kind of learning, well informed, quick to understand, and qualified to serve in the king's palace. He was to teach them the language and literature of the Babylonians. The king assigned them a daily amount of food and wine from the king's table. They were to be trained for three years, and after that they were to enter the king's service.

Daniel 1:3–5

In every matter of wisdom and understanding about which the king questioned them, he found them ten times better than all the magicians and enchanters in his whole kingdom.

Daniel 1:20

Everyone thinks of changing the world, but nobody thinks of changing himself [or herself].

Leo Tolstoy[11]

Where no attention is given to teaching, and to constant, lifelong Christian learning, people quickly revert to the worldview or mindset of the surrounding culture, and end up with their minds shaped by whichever social pressures are most persuasive, with Jesus somewhere around as a pale influence or memory.

Tom Wright[12]

'I wish it need not have happened in my time,' said Frodo. 'So do I,' said Gandalf, 'and so do all who live to see such times. But that is not for us to decide. All we have to decide is what to do with the time that is given us.'

From *Lord of the Rings* by J. R. R. Tolkien[13]

2

Avoid Early Graduation

There are some challenges in life that we probably don't anticipate.

Being slapped on the side of the head by flying fish that pummel you as you row, naked, across the Atlantic Ocean, is surely right up there when it comes to unforeseen circumstances.

In 2002, together with Andrew, her husband at the time, Debra Veal entered a competition to row a 24-foot-long plywood boat for 2,900 nautical miles in a transatlantic race. All seemed lost when, battling anxiety, Andrew abandoned the trip after just 14 days.

Debra decided to continue alone. The 111-day marathon was not just a physical challenge; it stretched her mental muscles to the limit. Some days she would row for hours, and then take a well-earned sleep break, only to find that she had drifted right back to where she'd started the day. Repetitive motion and friction meant that it was more comfortable to shed her clothing.

She battled waves that towered above her tiny craft, which was battered by force 8 squalls. Inquisitive sharks and looming supertankers bore down on her. Sleeplessness took its toll.

And then there were those flying fish.

In her inspirational book, *Rowing Alone*, Debra describes how she got through those long days that must have felt like an aquatic exile.[14]

One strategy involved sticking a Post-it note on the dashboard of her rowing cockpit.

Just three words were scrawled thereon.

Choose your attitude.

We might wonder how we would cope if life served up such a bewildering set of circumstances.

But then recently, we have all experienced a global bombshell, a season when the use of the word "unprecedented" has been, well ...

... unprecedented.

It has felt like a Bruce Willis disaster movie, except Bruce hasn't shown up yet to rescue the planet from that fast-approaching meteor, or in this case, the COVID-19 virus.

I'm writing this during the sad summer that none of us will ever forget, as the fight continues. I hope and pray that by the time you read this, the world will have succeeded in taming and corralling the vile germ.

In the early stages of lockdown we all experienced collective shock. Ordered to stay at home, everyday life came to a screeching halt. Deserted high streets and railway stations that once teemed with bustling shoppers and commuters gave an apocalyptic feel to the season.

Stay home. Save lives. Protect the NHS.

Devastated care homes. Tearful, exhausted medics. Hefty fines for walking the dog too far away from home. Massive hospitals constructed in weeks. Eye-watering unemployment figures and economic predictions. Tearful students outraged at examination result chaos.

We were all staggered. Bewildered.

How could this be happening?

We were all quickly and roughly shoved into a second choice existence. Nobody picks a pandemic.

Is this real, or am I going to wake up tomorrow and sigh with relief—it was all just a horrible dream?

Tragically, this was no fleeting nightmare, so we had to embrace new germ-warfare regimens: constant hand-washing, social distancing, hand gel everywhere, line up to shop, sign here if you enter a pub, work from home, clap the carers, be furloughed, navigate redundancy, worship online, don masks for shopping …

In short, we had to …

Adapt and learn.

Adaptation meant doing things in a way we'd never done them. We had to learn new skills. Working from home, forsaking the boardroom for the Zoom call. Juggling jobs with schooling at home. Adapt.

And that's exactly what Daniel and his friends did in their second choice home in Babylon. When you live there, adaptability and learning are not just useful.

They are vital for survival.

Writing about those who were most likely to live through the horrors of life in Nazi concentration camps, Paul Steinberg points to adaptability as a common trait among survivors: "To survive you had to try to adapt yourself—and be able to make the adjustment. Which right from the outset was impossible for highly structured personalities, men in their forties with social standing, a sense of dignity, men who couldn't accept that communication from on high to us, the bottom, came only through blows and insults."[15]

But Daniel and his friends didn't just survive in Babylon, which is good news, as they were to spend the rest of their lives there. They would have to navigate through some very challenging episodes that included lions and furnaces. But despite all the challenges, they flourished.

Young Daniel and his friends surely had hopes and dreams, perhaps shaped by their noble pedigrees, as we've seen. To state the obvious, nobody has ambitions about deportation.

The lads could have chosen to refuse any kind of assimilation into Babylonian culture, and as we'll see, there were lines they would refuse to cross. We rightly celebrate the unflinching heroes who won't budge an inch, who go to the flames rather than bow to pressure; we're surely humbled by the martyrs. But Daniel and his friends were willing to negotiate and compromise.

Perhaps another option was to settle into mediocre submission, sulky servitude. Doing the minimum to escape punishment or worse, they might have been resentful for the rest of their days, having been dislocated from everything that they held dear. They could have simmered into old age, bitter and twisted.

Life had hardly been fair. These were godly young men of principle who were not only exiled, but suffered because of the rebellion and sin of others.

Bad things happen to good people.

The writer of the book of Ecclesiastes was right in his complaint—the wicked often prosper while the righteous suffer. Some are born with a silver spoon of advantage; others begin life in poverty and face an uphill trek to break out of it. There are those who enjoy many years unspoiled by significant illness; others diligently exercise but die early because they inherited a cancer gene. We work long hours, going the extra mile for that employer, only to be made redundant in a ruthless culling to cut company expenditure. We almost danced down the aisle, excited about the adventure ahead, but the marriage cooled and then died. We read those Christian Christmas newsletters, and they bring pain. All those stories of perfect families, where the children (who play multiple musical instruments) take gap years to serve in missions and then land high-flying jobs in the city—we envy them because their successes torment us if our children didn't turn out as we had dreamed. We put our hard-earned savings into that golden investment opportunity, only to watch it vanish as we lose the wealth accumulated from a lifetime of work.

Life is not a bank, where those who diligently invest goodness can expect a dividend of trouble-free days.

Life isn't even fair, on this broken planet, for those who follow its Creator. Four thousand years ago, another youngster, Joseph, great-grandson of Abraham, suddenly found himself an exile because of his treacherous siblings. Envied because he was the family favorite, he was tossed into a pit, and trafficked into slavery. Like Daniel, he

would never return home again, his father duped into believing that
he'd perished.

Life started to improve, but then he was stalked by a powerful
sexual predator who falsely accused him of rape when he spurned
her advances. According to some Jewish commentators, he spent
twelve years in jail, forgotten by people he had helped.[16] Only after
more than a decade of pain and uncertainty did a new day of blessing dawn.

Life isn't fair.

That doesn't mean that we abandon the fight against injustice;
recognizing the injustices of the world doesn't give us an excuse for
passivity. We must work, pray, campaign, give, and speak to right
the wrongs where we can make an impact.

But Daniel and his friends were not paralyzed by the injustice
of their personal situation, even though they were forced to be
at someone else's beck and call. "Beck and call" is a fourteenth-
century phrase, meaning "to be entirely subservient to someone; to
be responsive to their slightest request." That was the day-after-day
situation for Daniel and his friends.

In their shoes, some would have shaken their fists at heaven,
either abandoning faith in God or settling into benign, vague belief.
Many of those exiled chose that pathway. Despite being warned by
prophetic voices that their national neglect of the covenant would
lead to judgment, they felt that God had abandoned them in their
darkest hour, and their flimsy faith was completely shattered.

But Daniel and his friends chose another pathway.

They adapted, retooling themselves for life in their new environ-
ment. They opted for flexibility rather than rigidity. Most Christians

view any form of compromise with suspicion and disdain. But the Hebrew Four picked their battles carefully.

When life serves up a season or series of second choices, there will be some aspects of life that are beyond our control, both positively and negatively.

The drawbacks were obvious, and I've already alluded to them.

On the plus side, the youngsters had some advantages that helped them in Babylon. We've already seen that they had probably come from a background of nobility that surely included privilege and wealth, and had afforded them a good education.

And then the young men were "handsome and without physical defect." In the ancient world, beauty was associated with intelligence. Studies suggest that the idea prevails today. According to an article published in *Business Insider*, attractive people experience a "beauty premium" in life:

> Studies show that you're more likely to get hired if you look well-groomed, that good-looking people make about 12% more money than less appealing folks, and that attractive real-estate brokers bring in more money than their less attractive peers. Indeed, according to a just-published paper on the 2018 congressional midterms, more attractive candidates are more likely to get elected.[17]

And we might be offended and irritated by the results of a Harvard study:

> When comparing women who wore makeup versus what they look like bare-faced, participants in a 2011 Harvard study viewed the groomed woman as more attractive, competent, likable, and trustworthy. "When inferring trustworthiness, likability, or competence from an image, we are influenced significantly not only by the attractiveness of the inherited phenotype but by the effects of the 'extended phenotype,' in this case, makeup," the paper states.[18]

It might surprise some to discover that this is true in the church world too. My observation is that handsome and beautiful Christian leaders have an advantage in ministry success. I make the observation as one who is not one of them, not being blessed with chiseled good looks, and often thought to be older than I am. Any influence that I've had for the kingdom has been despite my looks, not because of them. I'm not bitter.

While we might amend our appearance cosmetically (and, in our modern world, surgically), broadly, when it comes to looks, most of us get what we get. When life deports us to Babylon, we'd do well to decide what is beyond our control (and not waste time trying to change it), and instead consider where we might have the ability and freedom to bring change, and then give our full efforts to that.

To put it in the words of the rather hackneyed Serenity Prayer, used by Alcoholics Anonymous groups everywhere,

> God, grant me the serenity to accept the things I
>   cannot change,
> courage to change the things I can,
> and wisdom to know the difference.

Attributed to American theologian Reinhold Niebuhr, the prayer as he originally wrote it was:

"Father, give us courage to change what must be altered, serenity to accept what cannot be helped, and the insight to know the one from the other."

As we read about the Hebrew boys being enrolled in an enforced three-year study course in Babylonian thinking and culture, there are two ways to view their experience.

The first is to see it as an ominous attempt to eradicate their Jewishness.

Those selected for deportation were to undergo a thorough program of education and indoctrination: a virtual Babylonian brainwashing. They studied the literature and language of the Chaldean people. The subject matter included astronomy, mathematics, natural history, mythological literature, agriculture, and architecture. Although these young men were not being trained as soothsayers, but as upper-level administrators and advisors, nevertheless, the purpose of this curriculum was to change the way they thought: their worldview, their value system.

In what has been described as a "completely alien thought-world"[19] for the Hebrew boys, the Babylonians believed there were many gods, including a trinity of the most powerful, Anu, Enlil, and Ea. The lads would have been forced to study magic, astrology, and sorcery. This would have been a major challenge, because at this time in Jewish history, openness to the influences of other cultures would not have been encouraged. Day in, day out, these ideas would have been driven into the students' minds.

It got worse.

Archaeological evidence clearly shows that Daniel and his friends would have been taught the Babylonian practice of divination: predictions made by interpreting unusual terrestrial and celestial phenomena by examining sheep livers.[20] This kind of activity was clearly forbidden in Scripture. Daniel and his friends would have been very aware of Isaiah's prophetic warning:

"When someone tells you to consult mediums and spiritists, who whisper and mutter, should not a people inquire of their God? Why consult the dead on behalf of the living? Consult God's instruction and the testimony of warning. If anyone does not speak according to this word, they have no light of dawn" (Isa. 8:19–20).

They were being coerced into conformity.

And Babylonian culture was extremely arrogant. Babylon, being such an ancient city, was thought of as a city of destiny, a place of antiquity and mystique. Babylon was the place for winners, representing power and wealth gained by violent seizure, together with arrogance, pride and unbridled ambition. It represented a social system of oppression and exploitation ... that was incompatible with the worship of Israel's God at any level. Babylon, in Genesis 11, is the symbol of self-exaltation and revolt against God. Babylon's ambition was to become as great as God, to be independent of God.[21]

Babylon's proud boast was that they gained greatness because they knew what was what, about life and the universe. Nebuchadnezzar, the king, saw himself as more powerful than any god, including Israel's God. Later, when Shadrach, Meshach, and Abednego refused to bow the knee to his image and were threatened with swift cremation, he taunted them with the question, "What god will be able to rescue you from my hand?" (Dan. 3:15).

The Hebrew lads would have had the idea that the Babylonian worldview was *the* way, not *a* way, drilled into them.

Not good.

But now look at what happened from another camera angle.

This education program gave the youngsters a fast track opportunity to learn about their new world. They would discover why their overlords thought and acted as they did. If they were to thrive in the unfamiliar cultural system in which they found themselves, they needed to understand the system. They would have to learn how to be Babylonian. As Ernest Lucas says:

> Daniel refused to adopt a ghetto mentality in exile.
> He was ready to engage with this alien culture,
> even taking the opportunity to spend three years
> studying it to understand it in greater depth. He
> accepted a responsible job in its power structure.[22]

This was obviously not without risk: the possibility they would be seduced by what they were learning, their trust in the one true God eroded or eliminated. But Daniel and his friends opened their minds to these ideas yet, as their later behavior shows, not their hearts.

And in a sense, they had no choice but to enroll in the Harry Potter–like school. When your life is in the hands of a merciless despot, you don't rush to argue, although a life-threatening stand would come later.

They joined the class as commanded.

But we will see that they also set their sights on a greater objective: to come top of that class.

In telling us that the Hebrew Four were "showing aptitude for every kind of learning, well informed, quick to understand," the text uses Hebrew words that flow from the most common Old Testament word for wisdom. That description parallels the accolade that Pharaoh gave to Joseph when he appointed him prime minister: "there is no one so discerning and wise as you" (Gen. 41:39).

These bright, intelligent young men were being groomed to serve as advisors to the king. Their willingness to adapt and learn would bring huge opportunity.

I know what I know.
My God reigns.
We were warned by the prophets, the
ones that He spoke through.
Their words came true.
My God reigns.
But sometimes, in the small, shadowy
hours, I lie awake, and wonder.
These Babylonians are so
confident, so self-assured.
They are the winners, and credit
their gods for their success.
The city, the opulence, the power,
the world—they have it all.
They have me.
Day after day, we're told: our gods reign,
they say. Learn well, they say.
Yet, this I say, even as Jerusalem is a
smoking ruin, the temple destroyed.
Whatever I feel, whatever I sometimes
think, this I declare, sometimes a hundred
times a day, muttered under my breath:
My God reigns.

So what of us? As followers of Jesus, we follow the master of adaptation. In a way that we can't begin to understand without blowing
an intellectual fuse, Jesus, the agent of creation, adapts to being a
speck in a virginal womb; the very God of Gods shifts from heaven's
throne to a humble manger. As Erwin McManus says, "You can't
model your life after Jesus and be unwilling to adapt."[23]

A global leadership strategist, Blair Sheppard recently offered this
advice to parents: "What should we tell our children? That to stay
ahead, you need to focus on your ability to continuously adapt, engage
with others in that process, and most importantly retain your core sense
of identity and values. For students, it's not just about acquiring knowledge but about how to learn. For the rest of us we should remember
that intellectual complacency is not our friend and that learning—not
just new things but new ways of thinking—is a lifelong endeavor."[24]

Learning is what followers of Jesus do. Jesus said to His disciples, "learn from me" (Matt. 11:29), a call made to all who would
name themselves as His followers. The primary task of women and
men called to Christian leadership is teaching (Titus 1:9; 1 Tim.
3:2; 5:17; Heb. 13:7; Matt. 28:20).

And the call to discover and learn isn't canceled by the grave;
the journey of learning will continue. Being with Christ eternally
will enable us to discover and grasp more of God's grace and kindness. Writing to his friends in Ephesus, the apostle Paul describes the
wondrous future for those in Christ:

"And God raised us up with Christ and seated us with him in the heavenly realms in Christ Jesus, *in order that in the coming ages* he might show the incomparable riches of his grace, expressed in his kindness to us in Christ Jesus" (Eph. 2:6–7).

The word "show" here means to reveal. To whom will God "reveal" greater depths of His grace, as he uses our lives as working models? Perhaps there will be a grace academy for angels. They do have enquiring minds, and long to "look into" the ways that God's Word will be fulfilled, as the apostle Peter said, in 1 Peter 1:12: "Even angels long to look into these things."

Surely, we can assume that we will be part of the ongoing learning experience? Puritan preacher Jonathan Edwards, who intensely studied heaven, believed "the saints will be progressive in knowledge to all eternity."[25] But while learning will surely be forever, it's also lifelong. The academy is in session now. Are we still enrolled?

Life is about learning. We toddle and then walk because crawling is unsatisfactory; greeted with a box of assorted toys, the child tips the whole lot out at once because they don't want to miss anything.

Learners become innovators and inventors. Alexander Graham Bell is celebrated for giving us the telephone, which he invented at the age of twenty-nine. He could have stopped there, but he was endlessly curious, and went on to engage in a great variety of scientific activities involving kites, airplanes, tetrahedral structures, sheep breeding, artificial respiration, desalinization and water distillation, and hydrofoils. His "photo-phone" research provided the groundwork for our modern laser and fiber-optic communication systems.

Months before he died, Bell told a reporter, "There cannot be mental atrophy in any person who continues to observe, to remember what he observes, and to seek answers for his unceasing hows and whys about things."[26]

He was a lifelong learner par excellence.

New Christians are often voracious learners. Finding themselves in the totally unfamiliar territory of kingdom life, they are hungry for understanding. As a brand-new believer, armed (and sometimes dangerous) with a King James Bible containing beautiful, poetic language I could barely understand, I was keen to know. Courses designed to ground converts in the truths of the faith abound. But after a while, the learning grinds to a gradual halt: slowly, imperceptibly, we self-graduate.

We've read the Bible through a few times. We've heard a thousand sermons, sung ten thousand songs, attended the "breakthrough" conference. We're no longer open-mouthed and amazed at grace. While familiarity hasn't bred contempt, perhaps it's birthed a yawn.

As one Christian leader described it, we've "been there, done that, sung that."

We settle into sameness, faith becomes a dull habit, we're done exploring and asking questions. And some models of church almost encourage us to abandon any sense of inquisitiveness. Preaching and teaching should activate a search, not end it. Yet, as a preacher, I'm challenged by these words from Michael Frost (and think he might be overstating things a little, but the challenge is worthwhile):

> A lot of what takes place in pulpits and Sunday
> schools is really taking the search out of learning.
> We're too used to having the answers packaged
> for us. We're never asked to look. Our curiosity

is never pricked, our interest never aroused. We sit through sermons in a daze, half listening, lost in our own thoughts. When was the last time a sermon, a Bible study, or a Sunday school class got under your skin and activated such an interest that you felt compelled to meditate upon the matter, to research or explore an issue, to question others or to search for your own views? When sermons end, we close our Bibles. When was the last time you heard a sermon and went home and opened your Bible to discover more?[27]

Only lifelong learners can know the joy of singing in Babylon.

And like the Hebrew Four, we will need to listen to some voices that are unfamiliar, make us nervous, challenge our presuppositions, and might even intimidate.

He is seminary educated. His passion for the gospel is impressive. His sermons are constructed with meticulous attention to detail, a result of his disciplined approach to daily prayer. He attends conferences that he hopes will hone and sharpen his leadership skills. His children have been raised on a steady diet of Christian classics. They close each day with shared worship.

He is also deeply unpleasant to be around, has massive relational blind spots, and often alienates members of his church because of his rigidity. Part of a movement that is suspicious of any voices that don't represent their own views, he lives under the intolerable burden of being right all of the time. Unable to dialogue, most conversations with him turn into a one-sided monologue; when he does listen, it's usually just to pause for breath, which allows him to reload his verbal cannons for the next assault. He views conversations about theology as an opportunity to hunt for negative evidence, eager to spot something that needs correction. He has isolated himself from members of his closest family, who are Christians, but not the type of Christians that he approves of—and the approval list only includes Christians who believe what he believes, sing the songs that he sings, and approach life sharing his philosophy of life. With his study habits and courses and conferences, he looks like a learner, which he is not, for one simple reason: he only listens to voices that echo his own.

Like those proverbial birds of a feather that have a penchant for flocking together, we all have a tendency to find comfort by being with those who agree with us. We engage in mutual intellectual back-scratching, affirming our shared rightness and standing firm together against those who don't see things our way. We even dismiss them at high speed, not because we engage in debating and discussing (that's far too time-consuming), but because slapping them with the label "unsound" works well. Or we use the word "heretic," which is more devastating, because of its historical association with burning people alive in the name of God.

Sometimes diverse opinions are silenced by what sounds like a noble call to loyalty and unity. Wanting to be seen as a team player, we stifle our concerns, which may well be vital, and could prevent disaster.

Larry Kramer points out: "It's easy to preach to the choir, and even easier to be part of it. It's easy to surround ourselves with people who think as we do and to dismiss everyone who disagrees as stupid or corrupt. It's especially easy to act this way when our political leaders … relentlessly fan the flames of discord and contempt. Adopting a mindset when everyone else seems to be doing so is more than just easy. It's satisfying."[28]

In Babylon, those forced into the academy listened and learned from unfamiliar voices, and used that information and insight to gain influence in their second choice world. As we dialogue with those of a different mindset, we understand our mission field. As we read books written by those outside of our own preferred echo chamber, we allow what we think and believe to be proven in the furnace of critical evaluation. Truth can stand up to fierce interrogation, and the process will enable us to abandon false notions or strengthen our conviction in what is true.

We avoid an "us and them" attitude when we listen to dissonant voices. We use the muscle of our minds. Pride is banished as we embrace the humility needed to hear. We acknowledge that we are not always right.

If we only listen to voices that we find agreeable, disaster is inevitable.

Like the war in Vietnam.

His name was Robert McNamara. The first president of the Ford Motor Company to be from outside of the Ford family, he was made defense secretary by President John F. Kennedy. After Kennedy was murdered, Lyndon Johnson took the chair in the Oval Office. An insecure man who disliked debate, Johnson included McNamara in an exclusive three-person team that met every Tuesday, without any military advisors present. President Johnson didn't like opposing voices, firing three military aides because, as he put it, "They got in my way."

Johnson and his three advisors saw themselves as the inner cabinet, a family. Keen to maintain their position, the three advisors made sure they always agreed together on any advice they gave the president. In this setup, any disagreement was viewed as a threat, an act of disloyalty. McNamara went further, shielding Johnson from any dissident voices from within the chain of command in the wider administration. The president confirmed that he only wanted input through "the McNamara channel." The result? President Johnson made decisions in 1963 and 1964 that ultimately led to the futility of the war in Vietnam.[29] As Tim Harford says, "The right decisions are more likely when they emerge from a clash of very different perspectives."

In Babylon, Daniel and his friends adapted and learned, and as we'll see, their hard work would pay great dividends, not just for themselves, but for all their fellow exiles. But we've already acknowledged the risk. Would their studies and immersion in their new culture lead them to abandon their Jewish roots and become fully fledged Babylonians in thought, word, and deed?

FOR REFLECTION

1. What have you learned lately?

2. When was the last time you admitted that you were absolutely wrong about something?

3. How might you be being called to adapt in this current season of your life?

The chief official gave them new names: to Daniel, the name Belteshazzar; to Hananiah, Shadrach; to Mishael, Meshach; and to Azariah, Abednego.

Daniel 1:7

When all the people were being baptized, Jesus was baptized too. And as he was praying, heaven was opened and the Holy Spirit descended on him in bodily form like a dove. And a voice came from heaven: "You are my Son, whom I love; with you I am well pleased."

Luke 3:21–22

Jesus, full of the Holy Spirit, left the Jordan and was led by the Spirit into the wilderness, where for forty days he was tempted by the devil. He ate nothing during those days, and at the end of them he was hungry. The devil said to him, "If you are the Son of God, tell this stone to become bread."

Jesus answered, "It is written: 'Man shall not live on bread alone.'"

The devil led him up to a high place and showed him in an instant all the kingdoms of the world. And he said to him, "I will give you all their authority and splendor; it has been given to me, and I can give it to anyone I want to. If you worship me, it will all be yours."

Jesus answered, "It is written: 'Worship the Lord your God and serve him only.'"

The devil led him to Jerusalem and had him stand on the highest point of the temple. "If you are the Son of God," he said, "throw yourself down from here. For it is written:

"'He will command his angels concerning you
to guard you carefully;
they will lift you up in their hands,
so that you will not strike your foot against a stone.'"

Jesus answered, "It is said: 'Do not put the Lord your God to the test.'"

When the devil had finished all this tempting,
he left him until an opportune time.

Luke 4:1–13

We can find no period in Israel's history when she did not believe she was the chosen people of Yahweh … the prophets and the writers continually harped back to the Exodus as the unforgettable example of the power and grace of Yahweh, calling the people to himself. It is clear that from earliest times Israel saw herself as a people chosen by Yahweh and the object of his special favour.

John Bright[30]

3

Identity Theft

"My name is Jean Valjean!"

So cries the principal character in the brilliant musical play and film *Les Misérables*. Set in Toulouse, France, in 1820, Victor Hugo's classic story tells the story of Valjean, a thief who is reborn because of grace and kindness.

A prisoner on parole, yet branded by his past, Valjean is given food and shelter by a kindly clergyman, but rewards this hospitality by stealing some valuable silverware from the priest's home. Caught red-handed by the gendarmerie, he is stunned to hear the priest instruct the police officer to release him, insisting that the stolen candelabras were a gift, and giving Valjean some more silver, which, says the priest, "he had forgotten." Valjean is overwhelmed by such outrageous grace, and his life's direction is dramatically altered by that moment. Finally, he dies a good and godly man, beloved and serenaded by his adopted daughter and her husband, and summoned into the presence of God by a shimmering white angel. Not only has he vacated the prison, but he has also been set free from the cellblock of sameness—and all by the power of grace.

But in contrast, throughout his life he is hunted and threatened by his former captor, Javert. The bullying former prison guard and police inspector insists on calling Valjean simply by his number, 24601, even at the moment of parole. You are nobody, you're just 24601. Nameless and numbered, the despair in the chain gang is total. They pray, but then lament that Jesus doesn't care. In their second choice world, God, if He is there, has no interest in their plight.

When we are addressed by name, we feel included, noticed, valued. Our names matter. Conversely, when our name is not used, we feel objectified and anonymous. And if we lose the name we were given at birth, we are dislocated from our parents' choices; separated from our history.

In Albania, they took people's names very seriously. Right after the Second World War, the Communist authorities there required the substantial Greek population in southern Albania and other non-Albanians to "Albanize" their names. Citizens were ordered to give modern revolutionary (Illyrian) names to their children, while all over the country, non-Albanians who had names with religious connotations were "Albanized" with new names, better suited to the state ideology.

In the Ancient Near East, a person's name and identity were entwined in a way that we can't fully comprehend today. A name change could be viewed positively, especially if God was the One doing the renaming. Abram became Abraham, "father of many" (Gen. 17:5), while Abraham's wife Sarai, "my princess," became Sarah, "the princess and mother of nations" (Gen. 17:15–16). Jacob,

"the supplanter," became Israel, "he who has the power of God" (Gen.
32:28). Simon, "obedient," becomes Peter, "the rock" (John 1:42).
The combined name, "Simon Peter," which appears fifteen times in
the gospel of John and three times elsewhere, could be translated as
"Obedient Rocky." When the Hebrew Joseph came into the service
of the Pharaoh, he was given a new Egyptian name (Gen. 41:45).

Names spoke of destiny. In Hosea's story, his daughter was
named "Not-pitied," and his son was named "Not-my-people"
(Hos. 1:6–9). But later (Hos. 2:1, 23), the names were changed
to "My-people" and "She-was-pitied." The earlier names spoke of
Israel's rejection of God; the later names spoke of the promise of
God's forgiveness.

Those enrolled in the Babylonian program were given new
names, which, at first glance, honored the gods of Babylon. For
some enrolled in the program, this would be no problem; as I've
mentioned, many of those exiled were enraged, convinced that God
had abandoned them, so why shouldn't they forget Him?

The bitterness of the exile is captured in the desolation of
Psalm 137:

> Alongside Babylon's rivers
>   we sat on the banks; we cried and cried,
>   remembering the good old days in Zion.
> Alongside the quaking aspens
>   we stacked our unplayed harps;
> That's where our captors demanded songs,
>   sarcastic and mocking:
>   "Sing us a happy Zion song!"

Oh, how could we ever sing GOD's song
  in this wasteland?
If I ever forget you, Jerusalem,
  let my fingers wither and fall off like leaves.
Let my tongue swell and turn black
  if I fail to remember you,
If I fail, O dear Jerusalem,
  to honor you as my greatest.

GOD, remember those Edomites,
  and remember the ruin of Jerusalem,
That day they yelled out,
  "Wreck it, smash it to bits!"
And you, Babylonians—ravagers!
  A reward to whoever gets back at you
  for all you've done to us;
Yes, a reward to the one who grabs your babies
  and smashes their heads on the rocks![31]

For the four Hebrew youths, this renaming could represent a very real challenge, if the goal was to change their allegiance from Yahweh to the occult Babylonian gods.

The name Daniel means "Elohim is my judge." Elohim is one of the Hebrew names for God. Daniel's new name, Belteshazzar, means "May Bel protect his life." Bel is one of the gods of Babylon. Hananiah means "Yahweh is gracious." Yahweh is the personal name of the God of the Bible. Shadrach means "Aku is exalted," and Aku is another Babylonian god. Mishael means "Who is what

Elohim is?" while Meshach means "Who is what Aku is?" Azariah means "Yahweh is my helper," and Abednego means "The servant of Nebo," yet another Babylonian god.[32]

Some say that this renaming might not have been a deliberate attempt to degrade or humiliate, but the Hebrew Four had no choice in the matter. The occult roots of their new names must have rankled with their Jewish sensitivities. Giving new names was common court practice and was a sign of new ownership: you belong to me, now, and I'll call you what I want. And Meshach's name, comparing him to the might of a Babylonian god, also means "I am of little account." In direct contrast to this, Jesus gave a new name to Simon Peter, a name that spoke of rocklike reliability and hope.

The choice of the new names meant that honor was being paid to the four main gods of Babylon (although the strategy may have backfired, as we'll see later).

Babylon: this was the city based on the pursuit of a name: "We may make a name for ourselves" (Gen. 11:4).

The Hebrew Four came from a background where God Himself was the One who gave Adam and Eve their names, and who alone could make people like Abraham and his name great (Gen. 12:1–3). Now these Babylonian self-namers were handing out new names. This much is clear: the identity of the Hebrew Four was under serious threat.

Back in their homeland, the lads would have been constantly reminded of their unique identity in the purposes of God. The Lord, the great dramatist, used a vast number of props to creatively help Israel remember their great story of redemption and destiny.

The story was on their taste buds as God's people ate unleavened bread during the great Passover celebration.

Israel scribbled the story on the doorposts of her houses; she wore the story, tying symbols on her arms and forehead. She sang and danced the story, and preserved some of her miracle manna in a jar "for the generations to come" (Ex.16:33).

Altars and stone pillars were built, marking the sites of historic triumphs where God had helped His people. And there was high drama: Israelites had blood splashed over them as Moses read them the law.

The story was immortalized in construction by builders, and stitched and sewn by curtain-makers in the development of tabernacle and temple. Furniture-makers carved it exquisitely in wood, sculptors chiseled it, metalworkers hammered it out, and jewelers set the story in precious stones. The story was smelled in the wafting of incense; it was acted out through the theater of the elaborate sacrificial system. The priests were lead players in the drama, with their colorful vestments: the breastplate, turban, sash, and ephod. It was heard as the priestly bells jingled.

But the drama went further in the creation of the festivals and feasts. As God's people gathered together to remember and give thanks, those festivals and gatherings were opportunities for covenant renewal, evaluation, and definition. The Old Testament celebrations enabled the people of God to question themselves: Had they been faithful to the covenant? Where had they failed? Had they played their part and been faithful to the story?

And during the great festivals, the people reenacted their history creatively. They would not just hear the story rehearsed in words, but would participate in a huge play where they were the actors and audience both. The Passover feast was eaten by a people dressed ready for a journey, with cloaks tucked into belts, sandals on the feet, and a staff in hand. And a mass camp-out lasting seven days was required when the feast of the tabernacles was celebrated. It was not enough to hear about the nomadic journeying of their ancestors through the wilderness; the people lived in booths made of tree boughs and the branches of palm trees for seven days, to feel something of what their predecessors experienced.

Circumcision was the sign of covenant, the reminder of a union with God that made its mark on the very depths of the human psyche: faith impacting even that which is most private and usually hidden. Primarily it was a sign, a very real reminder, to the bearer of the mark: you are different. You belong to God.

Walter Brueggemann wrote: "Remember who you are by remembering whose you are. Be your own person in the face of empire, of the dominant ideology, of the great power of death. Be your own person by being in the company of the great God who works in, with, and through the training program of the empire for the sake of God's own people. Be your own person, because God has not succumbed to the weight of the empire."[33]

Back home, there were plenty of ways to stir memories and connect people with their big story. But now, in Babylon, Daniel and his friends had none of these cultural reminders—all that was gone, permanently. Perhaps one memory aid remained—the gold and silver vessels that had been taken from the temple in Jerusalem.

According to Ezra 1:11, there were 5,400 of them, perhaps stored in the Esagila temple, the treasure house, where Nebuchadnezzar's spoils of war were kept in what was like a museum to celebrate his triumphs. John Lennox wonders if Daniel and his friends fueled their faith with visits to that museum:

> One can imagine that Daniel and his friends went from time to time to the museum in order to admire the vessels that Nebuchadnezzar had taken from Jerusalem, and to reflect on their meaning. To them, those golden vessels that glittered on the display tables were holy, in the original sense of that word: they were vessels set apart for the glory of God. The gold from which they had been made was the most precious metal known at the time. In addition, gold was very hard to come by in Israel, so it was particularly suitable for expressing the glory of God and the fact that he was "the supreme value" (as we might say) of the nation. The temple vessels from Jerusalem had been made by craftsmen who loved God, as Daniel and his friends did.[34]

If they did, those artifacts were all that they had to remind them of their history, their story in God. The threat was obvious. If their identity was not to be obliterated, it might be systematically eroded.

Nothing's changed.

Our identity will come under attack as well.

In 1975, Michael Griffiths, then general director of the Overseas Missionary Fellowship, wrote a pithy and prophetic book with a telling title: *Cinderella with Amnesia*. He commented, "Christians collectively seem to be suffering from a strange amnesia. A high proportion of people who 'go to church' have forgotten what it is all for. Week by week they attend services in a special building and go through their particular, time-honoured routine, but give little thought to the purpose of what they are doing."[35]

It's all too easy for us to forget why we're here, to mislay our purpose, to lose sight of why we do what we do. But perhaps the problem goes deeper, to our actually forgetting who we are in Christ.

We know this, because we follow Jesus, and Satan tried very hard to undermine His identity. Notice the progression between Luke 3 and Luke 4. At baptism, Jesus' identity is affirmed by the Father: this is my Son. As Jesus begins His ministry by being baptized by John in the Jordan, and as He spends time talking with the Father, the heavens split open, and the Father speaks back.

What would you say to the One who is embarking on the greatest and most significant mission in the history of planet earth? Perhaps you'd assure them that you'd be with them all the way, or comfort them with a reminder that, although great pain was ahead, glory was in the future too. Instead the Father speaks but one sentence: "You are my Son, whom I love; with you, I am well pleased" (Luke 3:22).

Jesus hears His sonship celebrated, He is told that He is loved, and that the Father's pleasure is upon Him. Before we do anything for God, we need to do it from the place of knowing who we are in God. He is already pleased with us. Failure to grasp this will cause us to strive.

Immediately, in the wilderness, the devil tries to undermine Jesus' identity: "If You are the Son of God ..."

The satanic skirmishes came in three waves, and the first centered on Jesus' physical body. Contrary to what some preachers suggest, Jesus was not "God with skin on" but, in a way that is true yet beyond understanding, He was both fully God and fully man. After forty days without food, He was starving, literally. And so the question came: "If You are the Son of God ..." and then the invitation: prove Yourself.

Do a magic trick with bread, for Your own survival.

The devil's question amounted to this: "Who the hell do You think You are?"

The second temptation was about power. In return for an act of satanic worship, Jesus would know total earthly authority and be exalted, without having to go to the cross. And then the final attack came, complete with a misquoted portion of Scripture, as Satan suggested Jesus should throw Himself off the high pinnacle of the temple, which is believed to have been around 450 feet high.

Some ancient rabbis taught that when the Messiah would come and reveal Himself, He would stand on the roof of the temple.

Through a full-frontal attack, Satan tried to undercut and under-mine Jesus' identity. And he will do the same with us.

Our identity matters.

As we break bread, celebrate in worship, share in small groups, pray, and reflect on the truths of Scripture, we affirm that Christ is Lord, the only way, and we affirm that we belong to Him. We remember who He is, who we are, and whose we are.

It's just possible that the renaming backfired, and may have been a source of amusement to the young lads. Bible commentator John Goldingay suggests the names might have carried some subtle mockery of those gods:

"The wise person knows the power of laughter. The possibility that the outward renaming of the four Israelite young men might lead to their inner backsliding is undermined by the way their new names are reported. Belteshazzar, Shadrach, Meshach, and Abednego are all grotesque, silly names, which make fun of the gods whom they are supposed to honor."[36]

Some find it odd that Daniel and his friends didn't complain about those names, although if they were mocking the false gods, per-haps the group of lads decided that they were happy to be so named. Also, we should know that throughout the book of Daniel, the writer (probably Daniel himself) consistently misspells the new Babylonian names. And Daniel never refers to himself by his new name. It's as if he is sending us a message of subversion and even derision: "We cared so little about these ridiculous names, we couldn't even be bothered to spell them correctly as we recorded our story."

Perhaps also they felt that they needed to accept the names so they could be fully immersed in the three-year teaching and training program, and thereafter have influence. It's also possible that the renaming of the Hebrew Four may have consolidated their sense of togetherness in the face of such upheaval; sharing an experience, albeit painful, creates empathy and can consolidate. As we suffer indignity together, we bond; suffering can nurture closeness and community.

For whatever reason, they didn't fight about the renaming. Let's not be people who contest every issue, but pick our "battles" carefully and prayerfully.

You won't be going home, they said.
Not ever.
Forget your family. Forget the
landscape you once enjoyed.
Abandon your memories. Bury your
hopes, because you exist entirely to
serve someone else's agenda now.
You march to our drumbeat.
You have a pulse, but not a life.
And now, forget you, Daniel. Discard that
mad notion that your God cares about you.
Belteshazzar. That will be your
name from now on.

Your protector will be Bel, hence
your name, they said.
But you can call me what you
like, but inside, I'm Daniel.
My name is Daniel.
While I live, that's who I am.
You choose where I live.
If I live.
What I do.
What I'm called.
When I sleep.
You choose what I eat and drink.
Or do you?

FOR REFLECTION

1. What steps can you take to further deepen your identity in Christ?

2. Daniel didn't make an issue of everything. Have you "made a stand" about some issues in the past, only to realize that they were not so important?

3. If God were to give you a new name that reflects your strengths, what might the name be?

But Daniel resolved not to defile himself with the royal food and wine, and he asked the chief official for permission not to defile himself this way. Now God had caused the official to show favor and compassion to Daniel, but the official told Daniel, "I am afraid of my lord the king, who has assigned your food and drink. Why should he see you looking worse than the other young men your age? The king would then have my head because of you."

Daniel then said to the guard whom the chief official had appointed over Daniel, Hananiah, Mishael and Azariah, "Please test your servants for ten days: Give us nothing but vegetables to eat and water to drink. Then compare our appearance with that of the young men who eat the royal food, and treat your servants in accordance with what you see." So he agreed to this and tested them for ten days.

At the end of the ten days they looked healthier and better nourished than any of the young men who ate the royal food. So the guard took away their choice food and the wine they were to drink and gave them vegetables instead.

Daniel 1:8–16

Therefore, I urge you, brothers and sisters, in view of God's mercy, to offer your bodies as a living sacrifice, holy and pleasing to God—this is your true and proper worship. Do not conform to the pattern of this world, but be transformed by the renewing of your mind. Then you will be able to test and approve what God's will is—his good, pleasing and perfect will.

Romans 12:1–2

Now listen, you who say, "Today or tomorrow we will go to this or that city, spend a year there, carry on business and make money." Why, you do not even know what will happen tomorrow. What is your life? You are a mist that appears for a little while and then vanishes. Instead, you ought to say, "If it is the Lord's will, we will live and do this or that." As it is, you boast in your arrogant schemes. All such boasting is evil. If anyone, then, knows the good they ought to do and doesn't do it, it is sin for them.

James 4:13–17

Daniel teaches us that the struggle is not to make the culture Christian, but how a Christian can live in a hostile culture.

Tremper Longman[37]

4

Breaking Step

I feel rather sorry for lemmings.

They are creatures that have been much maligned.

Mention lemmings, and mass cliff jumping comes immediately to mind, because they're best known for hurtling over precipices in large numbers in what appears to be a bizarre suicide pact. The suggestion is that one of these critters gets it into his tiny brain that lobbing himself over a precipice would be a good idea, and all the other lemmings follow suit … like lemmings.

They are held in disdain for this perilous attitude of mindlessly going with the flow.

But apparently there is some reasoning behind all this free falling, because their behavior is more about relocation than a collective death wish. Lemming colonies experience population explosions every three or four years, and when that happens, a large group will head out in search of a new home. They are able swimmers, so when they reach a water obstacle such as a river or lake, they may try to cross it. Inevitably, a few drown. It's hardly suicide, but the idea persists, apparently given steam by Hollywood.

As I've written elsewhere,

The idea of mindless following was perpetuated by the 1958 Disney nature film *White Wilderness*. Some drama was required, and so, incredibly, filmmakers staged a lemming death plunge, pushing dozens of lemmings off a cliff as the cameras rolled. The images wrongly convinced several generations of moviegoers that these little rodents do, in fact, possess a bizarre instinct to destroy themselves. But there's a reason for their high diving. But we humans often have no reason at all for our herd-like behavior, as we get in step with everyone else simply because everyone else is marching in that direction. We humans are creatures of that herd. How quickly we emulate those we admire, and imitate those who are famous. We copy. Rather obviously, the fashion industry knows this. We buy what's hot, because someone, somewhere decides it's hot. Sometimes this verges on the ridiculous, as the practice known as "sagging" demonstrates. Some think that this trend, popularized by hip-hop artists in general and Justin Bieber specifically, originated from prison inmates being denied their belts to reduce risk of suicide. We mindlessly follow. And in recent years, this has become a very serious issue, and not just because of those chaps without belts who stagger around flashing their y-fronts. Now some of those who want to lead us over the cliff often insist that they are the only ones who are right, and we disagree with the crowd at our peril. Liberal fundamentalism rules. If I disagree with the popular consensus, then I'm quickly tagged as hateful or bigoted, one who must be silenced or banished immediately. It's ironic, because if we differ in our convictions and opinions, we're accused of being intolerant—and that won't be tolerated.[38]

Cardinal Ratzinger, who ultimately became Pope Benedict XVI, warned of a "dictatorship of relativism" in Europe. In a day where any attempt at founding life on absolute truth is viewed as dangerous, and where all that seems to matter is the right of the individual to pursue their own choices and appetites, the cardinal was right.

The Babylonian elite were foodies.

Babylon was a place of great feasting.

This would be a very luxurious mode of living for these Hebrew lads, quite in contrast to what they had been accustomed to, and to the extremely plain diet which Daniel requested for himself and his companions. The Babylonian kings and nobles were noted for their high living. Their tables were loaded with wheaten bread, meats in great variety, luscious fruits, fish and game. The usual beverage

was wine of the best varieties, and they were fond
of drinking to excess.[39]

It's possible that Daniel refused to eat and drink the king's food
because it had been offered to idols. Perhaps he chose an alternative
diet because he wanted to show the benefits of that choice. He was
certainly firm in his decision. We read, "But Daniel resolved …"
and the Hebrew word means "to appoint, commit, determine, hold,
purpose, wholly and steadfast."

Whatever the reason for his stand, notice that Daniel made a kind
request. Not only did he pick his battles, but he chose his tone carefully. We'd do well to emulate his measured approach, especially in
an age where we're tempted to issue capitalized rants in 140 charac-
ters or fewer. When we disagree, let's do so agreeably.

Notice too that Daniel asked permission about his *own* behavior,
and did not, in this instance, demand that everyone follow his example and comply with his convictions. Daniel did not even "go public"
with his diet decision—he just made a quiet diplomatic request.

Daniel and his friends were not deliberately looking for a fight.
Gerard Kelly comments:

> Able to pursue a path of non-conformity to the
> dominant values of Babylon, where these touch on
> matters of personal holiness and integrity, Daniel

and his friends do not go looking for trouble. They do not seem to see the "reform" of Babylonian culture as their priority, no matter how strongly we might want to "read this in" to the text. But they do pursue a life of quiet non-conformity, and are ready and willing to make a public stand whenever their non-cooperation is exposed. The goal of their non-conformity is that they must not "defile themselves" in Babylon (Dan 1:8). According to a framework of personal holiness to which we are not privy, they establish what the parameters of their non-conformity will be.[40]

Daniel's example suggests that we will always need to draw the line around who we worship, and how we should live in integrity and holiness. All followers of Jesus will, like Daniel, have to tread the pathway of non-conformity at times. Once again, this is because of our identity as Christ followers.

But let's remember that we are not told why Daniel made those choices. While the Bible is very clear about some standards of behavior, personal choices in ethical matters that are not specifically covered by biblical teaching will differ. Each of us needs to figure out where the "lines" are for ourselves. If we don't recognize this, we will descend into mindless legalism. As Walter Brueggemann states:

Daniel prevailed over exile, and in the process, he maintained freedom in his faith. He did not conform. He did not attempt to gain or enhance his

worth by conforming, nor to save his life by keeping
it. Sustained by faith, Daniel is his own man as he
is God's man, and he does not conform. The text
is not, I submit, remote from our own situation in
which pressures in church and society to conform are
great. We imagine our worth comes in conforming,
in unquestioning obedience, in responding quickly
to every opinion poll of preference. The conforming
happens subtly, not frontally. We join the dominant
ideology with innocence and without noticing. In
the congregation are those who do not notice their
conformity and thus are incapable of imagining any
alternative. We may notice how "the others" have
conformed; we are not so skillful in noticing how we
ourselves have joined the version of ideology most
compatible with our social location and interest.[41]

It seems like madness.
Nobody refuses the king's provision.
Nobody.
If our guard reports us, everything is lost.
But something in me compels me.
The food is delicious, the best, but we can't eat it.
It's not that it turns my stomach.
It turns my heart.

When I first made the approach, and our guard
turned me down, I was tempted to walk away.
Shrug my shoulders.
I'd done my best. Made my stand. Nobody
could blame me for backing off now.
Surely God would understand my predicament.
But then, I pushed the matter harder, wondering
if my persistence might cost me …
Everything.
Impossibly, I made a deal.
Test me, test us.
And so that's the agreement.
And now?
We will see.
God, help us.

Increasingly, Christians are coming under pressure to conform. In our culture, the current challenge is not so much about our desire to worship Christ as Lord.

The conflict often arises when we rightly insist that Christ is the *only* God and we are choosing to live life His way. As we've seen from Daniel's example, this does not give us the right to demand everyone must also live this way, even though, as we'll see, God's way is for all humanity and is the best way! But we need to remember the pressure we face is nothing new.

Gerard Kelly writes:

> It is all too easy to perceive that the pressure on
> Daniel to give into the worship of idols and abandon
> the worship of Yahweh is different to the pressures
> we face today. Sixth century Babylon was remark-
> ably similar to today's postmodern pluralist culture.
> Babylon offered all kinds of worship to all kinds
> of gods; eight city gates where named after differ-
> ent gods; different temples to different gods existed
> simultaneously in the city. Daniel was not under
> pressure to worship a particular pagan god so much
> as to go along with the pluralism that allows for any
> and all gods. You can pray to Yahweh if you wish,
> just as long as you do not make his worship exclu-
> sive. To resist this pressure, insisting on his God's
> claim to exclusive worship, was to live in faithfulness
> to the long-standing Old Testament rejection of all
> idolatry. For Daniel, as for us, the issue was not only
> the freedom to worship Yahweh; it was the freedom
> to worship Yahweh as the only God. A faith in
> which our God is one god among many is unlikely
> to be challenged in a pluralist, tolerant culture, but a
> faith in which our God demands exclusive worship
> will lead us unavoidably to noncompliance.[42]

We've seen that Daniel may have refused the king's food because
of its association with idols. This episode can seem irrelevant to

us—but we can be tempted to create and worship idols too. Tremper Longman writes:

> At first it is difficult for us as modern Christians ... to identify with the challenge facing the Jewish people on the plain of Dura. But ... the issue transcends the worship of a particular statue and concerns instead the worship of the true God by elevating anything or anyone else to a comparable place of importance in our lives. As John Calvin provocatively charged, the human mind is a "factory of idols." We are constantly, even as Christians, in a struggle with this temptation.[43]

We humans are wired for worship and, as Bob Dylan made clear, we are all going to have to serve someone.

Who or what are we serving?

As we've seen, the culinary delights of Babylon must have presented significant temptation for the Hebrew lads. They had the opportunity to eat and drink the finest food and wine in the land, courtesy of the royal household. But all that glitters is not gold, and sometimes what seems so attractive is not so good after all—if in doubt, ask Adam and Eve. The diet the Hebrew Four chose was basic, but when "tested," they looked healthier and more nourished than those who had been feasting at the royal table. God's way is best.

Just in practical, healthy terms, living God's way makes perfect sense, because He is the designer and Creator, and knows what is best for us. There have been studies—including one that originated in Harvard—that suggest faith generally and church attendance specifically lead to a healthier life—some even say a longer life, by up to four years. Unsurprisingly, these reports are disputed, and while we shouldn't place too much reliance on them, there are obvious benefits to Christian discipleship.

God's commands to us are not to stifle life, but to enable us to live as we truly should—and we and those around us benefit as we walk in His ways. As we share in church community, we can defeat loneliness and grow through relating to each other, and caring for each other. As we pray, we have the opportunity to deal with worry as we share our cares with the God who cares and intervenes. In a bingeing culture, moderation creates health, prevents drink-driving, and alcohol-fueled violence.

Sexual purity is another example: God, who created us, knows how best to provide for us because He knows how He has wired us (Ps. 139:14). Therefore, His commandments are good for us … if we choose not to follow God's ways in the area of sexuality, we will suffer the negative consequences of our actions because we are going against our natural design. God's way is best because, as the epistle of James celebrates, He has the franchise on good and perfect gifts (James 1:17).

A commitment to faithfulness may call for us to remove things from our lives, as well as doing our very best. It's been noted that filmmaker Walt Disney was ruthless in cutting anything that got in the way of a story's pacing, even when a lot of time and money had been spent on creating that element of the movie. It's been said that one of the animators for *Snow White* recalls working 240 days on a four-and-a-half-minute sequence that Disney thought funny, but he decided the scene stopped the flow of the picture, so it was cut.

Are there habits or lifestyle choices that we need to cut?

The child, firmly told that they cannot play near that open third-floor window, stomps off and refuses to cooperate; their anger is their response to being denied what they want. Something similar could have happened in the hearts of Daniel and his friends; they could have taken the view that God had not spared them from exile, so why should they serve Him anyway? Also, they were nine hundred miles from home—nobody back there knew how they were living, and they could have become careless. But they were obedient to what they felt was being asked of them.

Daniel and his friends were not just faithful in their youth, but for decades. Faith and faithfulness are for life—until Christ comes or calls. Let's heed Daniel's example, and the warning from the epistle of James, urging those of us who have given our lives to Jesus to make sure that we don't gradually take them back again (James 4:13–17).

Despite facing the awful horrors of the cross, Jesus went "all the way" with the will of His father. He is our "faithful High Priest." Speaking of faithfulness, Richard Patterson says:

> The greatest example, of course, is that of Jesus Christ. Already as a child on one occasion (Luke 2:49) he asked his parents, "Didn't you know that

I must be" in the [things] of my Father? (or "about
my Father's business,") … During his earthly
ministry he taught the need for faithfulness (cf.
Matt. 25:21–23; Luke 16:10), a faithfulness that
he himself exemplified (cf. Heb. 3:1–6). Therefore,
as the time for him to crown his faithful ministry
by the laying down of his life drew near, he could
testify to the Heavenly Father, "I glorified you on
earth by completing the work you gave me to do"
(John 17:4). It is not surprising, then … that in his
return to judge the earth John foresees that he will
be called, "Faithful and True" (Rev 19:11).[44]

In Babylon, may we be found faithful, especially when we're
called to break step with the madding crowd.

FOR REFLECTION

1. Babylon demanded that Daniel and his friends conform. How
might our culture demand that of us today?

2. Daniel didn't make an issue of everything. What issues matter?
Where might we be called to "make a stand"?

3. Daniel cut out choice foods from his diet. What areas of your life
might require some self-pruning?

To these four young men God gave knowledge and understanding of all kinds of literature and learning. And Daniel could understand visions and dreams of all kinds. At the end of the time set by the king to bring them into his service, the chief official presented them to Nebuchadnezzar. The king talked with them, and he found none equal to Daniel, Hananiah, Mishael and Azariah; so they entered the king's service. In every matter of wisdom and understanding about which the king questioned them, he found them ten times better than all the magicians and enchanters in his whole kingdom. And Daniel remained there until the first year of King Cyrus.

Daniel 1:17–21

This is the text of the letter that the prophet Jeremiah sent from Jerusalem to the surviving elders among the exiles and to the priests, the prophets and all the other people Nebuchadnezzar had carried into exile from Jerusalem to Babylon. (This was after King Jehoiachin and the queen mother, the court officials and the leaders of Judah and Jerusalem, the skilled workers and the artisans had gone into exile from Jerusalem.) He entrusted the letter to Elasah son of Shaphan and to Gemariah son of Hilkiah, whom Zedekiah king of Judah sent to King Nebuchadnezzar in Babylon. It said: This is what the LORD Almighty, the God of Israel, says to all those I carried into exile from Jerusalem to Babylon: "Build houses and settle down; plant gardens and eat what they produce. Marry and have sons and daughters; find wives for your sons and give your daughters in marriage, so that they too may have sons and daughters. Increase in number there; do not decrease. Also, seek the peace and prosperity of the city to which I have carried you into exile. Pray to the LORD for it, because if it prospers, you too will prosper."

Yes, this is what the LORD Almighty, the God of Israel, says: "Do not let the prophets and diviners among you deceive you. Do not listen to the dreams you encourage them to have. They are prophesying lies to you in my name. I have not sent them," declares the LORD. This is what the LORD says: "When seventy years are completed for Babylon, I will come to you and fulfill my good promise to bring you back to this place. For I know the plans I have for you," declares the LORD, "plans to prosper you and not to harm you, plans to give you hope and a future. Then you will call on me and come and pray to me, and I will listen to you. You will seek me and find me when you seek me with all your heart. I will be found by you," declares the LORD, "and will bring you back from captivity. I will gather you from all the nations and places where I have banished you," declares the LORD, "and will bring you back to the place from which I carried you into exile."

Jeremiah 29:1–14

I thank Christian and other faith communities and faith organisations for the work they do in our communities supporting the vulnerable and oppressed …
the work that Christians and all church and faith communities across the UK do is invaluable to so many. The way in which you stand against injustice in all its forms, and support the poor and the needy, represents the very best of the Christian faith.

Jeremy Corbyn[45]

5

Blessing Babylon

It was one of the most poignant and powerful Christian gatherings of my entire life. That's a big statement to make, because I've sat through quite a few.

There were no big crowds.

Just fifteen or so people were there, yet the worship was breathtaking, the preaching nothing short of epic, the prayers electrifying. Jesus was there, surely smiling. And so was Santa Claus, splendid in a rich red coat lined with snow-white fur. It was an emotional evening; laughter and tears mingled. I even spotted Santa quietly sobbing.

The event was Hope's baptism. She was just eleven, and she was suffering from osteogenic sarcoma, a cancer of the bone. The prognosis was bleak. Save a miracle, there would be just days left. Hope had bravely battled the disease for eighteen months.

Hope and her family know pain. Two years before that baptismal evening, Hope's dad had died at an impossibly young thirty-eight, struck down by colon cancer. Now Hope's mum, Diane, is married to lovely Justin, all smiles and care and support.

And so that night we gathered, parents, grandparents, siblings, and friends, to enable Hope to declare her faith through baptism. She was bright and bubbly, and looked completely healthy. Her smile was like daybreak, a dawning sun that sends shadows packing.

The sermon lasted just three minutes; perhaps more should.

Diane, her lovely daughter smiling up at her, told us Hope believed in miracles, but she was not afraid of death. Hope nodded, peace and joy entwined in her. Diane told us life is but a mist, the Bible says, and soon we'll all be together. There was no schooled bravado, no rehearsed, rigid religiosity: just faith that bubbled over, like clear, cold water on a Sahara day. As Diane baptized her daughter, it was surely a priceless act of worship that shook and stirred the heavens.

Then came the prayers. First, Hope's brothers and sisters prayed out loud, their clear voices thanking God for the gift of her:

Please, Lord, please.

Let her stay longer.

And then Hope prayed; no child spiritual prodigy this, just a little girl with faith.

"Jesus, thank You for my family and friends. You are an awesome God. I just want Your will for me. I love You, Jesus. Amen."

I had determined to hold it together. I quietly failed, shoulders shaking.

Finally came the goodbyes, and the gargantuan grace that is usually only found among those who have suffered much. The family thanked us for coming, kindness from broken hearts, perhaps unaware of the sign and the wonder that they had just shared with us.

It was then that Santa cried. Isabelle, Hope's little sister, was all dressed up for Christmas, in her gorgeous red Santa dress. Her smile was broad too, with the chaotic teeth that make a seven-year-old so delightful. Now, as she hugged her mother tight, tears brimmed over her eyes.

And as we stepped out into the crisp Colorado chill, I remembered that Christianity really is about our forever. Our message is that, whatever hellish bullets life throws at us, there is a God, tough to understand at times, but utterly reliable to trust. Death, hell, pain, tears: in the end, He's beaten the lot, and we should remember that daily. Someone has said we can be too heavenly-minded to be of any earthly use. They were quite wrong. There's never been a human being in history who was too heavenly-minded.

Thank you, Hope. At just eleven, you fully lived up to your name, little lady. That evening, with you, we shared faith, worship, joy, and grace.

Shortly after her baptism, Hope passed away. Some years went by. And then Hope's sister, Isabelle, bright and beautiful at just nineteen, passed away too, another victim of that cursed cancer gene. And now brother Slate is courageously dealing with leukemia.

So, consider Diane. She lost her first husband, and now two of her children have gone ahead of her in death. If there was ever a family that has lived in a second choice world, it is the Hermann family.

But look again. The grief is real, raw, awful. But it is not paralyzing because, fueled by the resurrection hope of Christ, Diane, Justin, and Slate are spending themselves serving. They founded and lead the House of Hope, Guatemala, a place of rescue and healing for abandoned and abused children.

Ivan is one of those children. Raised in a brothel, he had been kept caged in a dog kennel with pets. When he arrived at the House of Hope orphanage, he was terrified. Diane describes "an amazing softness" that eventually came over Ivan.

And then there's Chayo, one of the first little girls to come to the House of Hope. Arriving as a two-year-old, she was covered in vomit and diarrhea, with a raging temperature of 104 degrees. She screamed continuously for around three weeks. She was completely deaf in one ear and 80 percent deaf in the other. Everyone in the home learned sign language, and eventually money was raised for an implant. Her life has been totally changed. She is safe, has hope, and will learn about the love of God in Christ. And all because a family, so battered and bruised by the evil predator that is cancer, determined to serve in the midst of their pain.

When we find ourselves in a second choice life, at the risk of sounding brutal, let's not live the rest of our days curled up in a me-centered ball.

God is revealed as a giver in Babylon. It was the Lord who gave the chief official sympathy toward Daniel and his friends. Now God gives again, granting the four Judeans "knowledge and understanding." As servants of the divine Giver, Daniel and his friends gave themselves to study and, as they did, God gave not only knowledge, but Daniel was gifted to understand and interpret dreams.

God gave.

Daniel and his friends gave.

When we find ourselves in Babylon, may we know grace that enables us to serve and give.

Imagine how you might feel.

Rudely thrust, not only into a location that is not your home, you learn that you have been enrolled in that three-year training course that we considered earlier. Viv Thomas comments:

> Daniel and his friends threw themselves into this Babylonian second choice experience. In one way or another they were clearly committed to Babylon. They poured themselves into it, even though they did not want to be there and it was all that they might easily have found "impossible." They worked so hard and well that they surpassed their Babylonian contemporaries in the process; those for whom Babylon was the first choice world. The Hebrews demonstrated "wisdom" and "understanding"—and all in the service of an institution and culture which was totally alien to their own. For the Hebrews "wisdom" was not just about being smart or clever; it was always associated with godliness and carried the sense of living responsibly before God. These Hebrews gave the very best

they had received from God and they gave it to an
anti-God community. It is possible that their major
drive was to avoid death and they knew that the
best way to do that was to serve enthusiastically,
but that doesn't seem likely; as the story shows,
they were ready to face death at any time. It was
a remarkable process and one which challenges all
of us. Rather than avoiding or running from their
second choice world they pursued it and gave it the
very best they had. They headed for the center of
the volcano, the heart of the storm, the vortex of all
their fears. For these men, the way to face Babylon
was to become skilled and powerful insiders, not
"separated" outsiders. When they chose this way
they rejected pouting, self-pity, resentment and
self-consumption. The fact that Babylon was a place
of dislocation, pain and disappointment did not
compel them to make a negative response to this
pagan world. Being servants of God in Jerusalem
or Babylon alike demanded living well before him.
It is as people watch us go through our second
choice world and do it well that the subversion
takes place. How we cope with disappointment,
how we respond to suffering, how we react to losing dignity and how we cope with authority—all
speak with compelling eloquence to a needy world.
We live in a world where people do not trust the
media, and are constantly bombarded by messages

which seek to separate them from their money. In a world which continually puts pressure on people to change their alliances or value systems the crying need is for authenticity. Second choice worlds open up the opportunity for seeing that authenticity demonstrated.[46]

None of us wants this opportunity.

When tragedy strikes, we don't want to be an example. We want to escape it, move forward out of the storm into more summery circumstances.

If God wants working models, let Him choose someone else.

But the story of Daniel shows us that not only did Daniel and his friends give themselves to the hard work of acquiring knowledge and understanding, but they were better than any of the homegrown talent. The text emphasizes that with two superlative descriptions of the Hebrew Four—the king "found none equal to Daniel, Hananiah, Mishael and Azariah," and then, to ensure that we get the message, "In every matter of wisdom and understanding about which the king questioned them, he found them ten times better than all the magicians and enchanters in his whole kingdom."

In short, they were the best of the best.

It was one of the funniest moments in the history of *Monty Python's Flying Circus.* Someone poses the question, "What have the

Romans ever done for us?" suggesting that nothing good had ever come from that empire. Eventually, after a long list of benefits, he retorts by agreeing that the Romans had brought massive improvements, but still poses the same question: What have the Romans ever done for us?

Sometimes a similar attitude is shown toward the Christian church—what good has come from her? And we can and should blush with shame when we look back at some of the hideous acts perpetuated in the name of God: the burning of heretics, philandering and murderous popes, the Crusades, turning a blind eye toward racism, apartheid and slavery, oppressing women, selling indulgences, and supposedly offering more immediate access to heaven for those with the means to pay for it. The list of horrendous acts is long.

But then look again.

The church has given teaching that helped shape the welfare state in the UK and elsewhere, and offered the world a better view of marriage, sexuality, and family life. In certain places, she helped outlaw the horror of human sacrifice, infanticide, and polygamy. She has been a primary provider of education and health care in many countries, preserving literacy in Western Europe when the Roman Empire collapsed. The church founded many great universities, and gave the world some staggering architecture. Artists, composers, and philosophers have been inspired by her.

Less obviously, Christianity has profoundly affected music, and not just through Gregorian chant and the work of Bach. As Mike Starkey points out: "The most popular forms of music in the world today—hip-hop, and the myriad varieties of dance music—have roots in the soul and funk that grew directly out of the black churches.

The musical legacy of black Gospel is vast, and has unquestionably shaped the world my teenagers inhabit."[47]

According to a review of Nobel prizes awarded between 1901 and 2000, 65.4 percent of Nobel Prizes Laureates have identified Christianity in its various forms as their religious preference.

Just as Daniel and his friends were invaluable in their second choice world, so we need to humbly but confidently affirm that we do and can bring so much that is needed in our day. With God's help, we who follow Christ can bless Babylon.

What do we bring today?

As Daniel did, we can bring the wisdom of God. We claim to personally know the One who designed the universe and everything in it, the One who knows how everything works best. We offer principles about marriage, truths about friendship. There are dynamic money management principles found in Proverbs.

We have practical teaching that can aid forgiveness and reconciliation; when South Africa ended the evil system of apartheid, she turned to the church to help with the process of healing, with the Truth and Reconciliation Commission headed by Bishop Desmond Tutu. We offer principles of harmony that can make the workplace better for employer and employee.

We provide insight on leadership, because Christian leaders are called to empower volunteers. Voluntary service has a financial value to the American economy of $24.69 per hour, which is equivalent to $297.5

billion/year. In the UK, the voluntary sector contributed £18.2bn to the economy in 2017–18, representing about 0.9 percent of total GDP.

But leading volunteers can be tricky, because they can't be motivated by a paycheck or chastened by the possibility of demotion or redundancy:

> It's crucial that organizations harness the energy, talent and time of volunteers in the most effective way. Even though volunteers have typically self-elected to give of themselves, they can be unreliable, inconsistent, and often easily become disengaged. Why is this? After all, they've offered to help of their own volition. Ultimately, it's because people have to fit volunteerism into an ever shifting puzzle of competing priorities and demands within both their professional and personal lives. Sometimes, the realities of those demands understandably take precedence. Solving the puzzle of volunteer fit and consistent engagement has more to do with how they are managed, and more importantly, led.[48]

We present a life with purpose, one worth sacrificing for, the answers to many mysteries, the ability to trust when we don't understand, to endure when life is toughest.

We offer truth: not "my truth" or "your truth." Something is either true or it is not. Martyrs suffered agonizing deaths and others endured years of solitary confinement because they refused to abandon the truth of Christ.

We provide the possibility of the supernatural and the miraculous. Freedom from addiction. Divorce counseling. Our buildings are used to serve our communities. Crèche facilities, youth groups, community meeting places, fitness classes, adult education courses, charity events, food banks, and coffee mornings are all served by the locations we offer.

Supremely, we bring good news, the gospel.

We bring the meaning of life, we point to the source of everything good, the solution to shame, we speak of the way things should be. We are signposts to forever. In a world spinning out of control, God is. We bring a reason for environmental responsibility as good stewards of a planet that was only ever lent to us. Just as the Jews viewed the law as a beautiful gift, we bring the inspired Word of God, holding out the Word of Life.

We have influence. In our workplaces. Our families. Our friendships. Our casual interactions with the checkout person at the store. With the neighbor whose company we enjoy. With the neighbor who drives us mad. At the school gates. At the health club. In the parent-teacher association. In our church. In our volunteering opportunities. With those we lead. With those who lead us. At the edge of the football field, as we stand with other parents watching those kids kick a ball.

Yes. We too can serve and bless Babylon.

Some would say we are mad.

Others would be quick to tag us as

traitors, lackeys of the enemy.

We should hate them, do everything

we can to subvert them.

Smile, comply, but quietly scheme and

collaborate to at least cause them grief.

But there's a strange inner

compulsion that we feel.

They have cursed us, but we will bless them.

In their strength, they have taken everything

we have, but we will work …

to make them stronger.

Why?

Perhaps it's this.

We serve, not them, but God. What we

do for them is worship toward Him.

Who knows?

As we give our best, light might shine.

And so, confused, and sometimes

with quiet raging within,

We will pray for Babylon.

We will bless Babylon.

FOR REFLECTION

1. How are you and your church "blessing Babylon"?

2. Daniel and his friends were renowned for their excellence. Which areas of your life do you think you could improve?

3. Has pain led you to opt out of serving and purpose, and now you need a change of direction and attitude? If so, how do you believe you could move forward?

In the second year of his reign, Nebuchadnezzar had dreams; his mind was troubled and he could not sleep. So the king summoned the magicians, enchanters, sorcerers and astrologers to tell him what he had dreamed. When they came in and stood before the king, he said to them, "I have had a dream that troubles me and I want to know what it means."

Then the astrologers answered the king, "May the king live forever! Tell your servants the dream, and we will interpret it."

The king replied to the astrologers, "This is what I have firmly decided: If you do not tell me what my dream was and interpret it, I will have you cut into pieces and your houses turned into piles of rubble. But if you tell me the dream and explain it, you will receive from me gifts and rewards and great honor. So tell me the dream and interpret it for me." Once more they replied, "Let the king tell his servants the dream, and we will interpret it."

Then the king answered, "I am certain that you are trying to gain time, because you realize that this is what I have firmly decided: If you do not tell me the dream, there is only one penalty for you. You have conspired to tell me misleading and wicked things, hoping the situation will change. So then, tell me the dream, and I will know that you can interpret it for me."

The astrologers answered the king, "There is no one on earth who can do what the king asks! No king, however great and mighty, has ever asked such a thing of any magician or enchanter or astrologer. What the king asks is too difficult. No one can reveal it to the king except the gods, and they do not live among humans."

This made the king so angry and furious that he ordered the execution of all the wise men of Babylon. So the decree was issued to put the wise men to death, and men were sent to look for Daniel and his friends to put them to death.

When Arioch, the commander of the king's guard, had gone out to put to death the wise men of Babylon, Daniel spoke to him with wisdom and tact. He asked the king's officer, "Why did the king issue such a harsh decree?" Arioch then explained the matter to Daniel. At this, Daniel went in to the king and asked for time, so that he might interpret the dream for him.

Then Daniel returned to his house and explained the matter to his friends Hananiah, Mishael and Azariah. He urged them to plead for mercy from the God of heaven concerning this mystery, so that he and his friends might not be executed with the rest of the wise men of Babylon.

Daniel 2:1–18

It is better to remain silent and be thought a fool, than to open your mouth and remove all doubt.

Abraham Lincoln

To be resident but alien is a formula for loneliness that few of us can sustain. Indeed, it is almost impossible to minister alone because our loneliness can too quickly turn into self-righteousness or self-hate. Christians can survive only by supporting one another through the countless small acts through which we tell one another we are not alone, that God is with us. Friendship is not, therefore, accidental to the Christian life.

Stanley Hauerwas[49]

The Germans' psychological methods often failed. They tried to get the inmates to think only of themselves, to forget relatives and friends, to tend only to their own needs … but what happened was just the reverse. Those who retreated to a universe limited to their own bodies had less chance of getting out alive, while to live for a brother, a friend, an ideal, helped you hold out longer. As for me, I could cope thanks to my father. Without him I could not have resisted. I would see him coming with his heavy gait, seeking a smile, and I would give it to him. He was my support and my oxygen, as I was his.

Elie Wiesel[50]

6

First Responders

It was such a depressing sight.

In the early days of the 2020 viral lockdown, two ninja-shoppers in a London Asda had to be pulled apart. Their fury was not because they had traded insults or had a shopping cart collision. One of them had bagged the last available package of toilet tissue, and that was the last straw. Similar scenes broke out around the world.

Psychologists scratched their heads. There was no suggestion that catching the virus led to a need for more toilet paper, yet shoppers were stripping the shelves like frenzied piranhas circling a dead cow. Some speculated the toilet paper mania was associated with cleanliness; just as hand gel nukes bacteria, so apparently having clean nether regions gains greater importance in a germ-ridden crisis. But others saw the panic buying as an expression of control. Professor Karestan Koenen said, "When you're seeing extreme responses, it's because people feel like their survival is threatened and they need to do something to feel like they're in control."[51]

But here's what happened when we took things into our own control.

The shops and stores sold out. The panic-buying fulfilled its own prophecy, and supplies ran short, hence the thuggish behavior of some shoppers.

As our recent history shows us, when we feel in peril, thoughtless panic can seem like the most reasonable reaction.

In the story of Daniel and his friends, before they tamed any lions, before anyone emerged from furnace-hot flames, something close to miraculous occurred.

The king was losing sleep, traumatized by a series of nightmares. We'll consider that dream in greater detail later, but for now, let's just know that it included a mixed media statue made of gold, silver, bronze, iron, and clay. The statue was pulverized by a rock. In the ancient world, where people believed that the gods broadcasted warnings using dreams, this seemed ominous indeed.

But the royal household had a team of occult specialists on permanent standby for situations like these. They would consult their dream manuals (some of which have survived) and offer an interpretation. They just needed to know the content of the dream. Wary that his advisors might try to scam him, however, the king made a decision.

He wasn't telling.

The royal dream team protested. What the king demanded was impossible. And that did not go down well with the most powerful man in the ancient world. They were condemned to a horrible death.

And again, in a world that's not fair, Daniel and his friends were included in the sentencing.

Their fate was signed, sealed, and about to be delivered. The warrant for their execution had been issued. Condemned to die by being cut into pieces, this meant they would be dismembered, either hacked to death or stretched out and pulled apart, a common practice at the time. The king had recruited a guard of men who also doubled as executioners; some believe they were former butchers, skilled in the use of the meat cleaver.

Daniel would know this was no idle threat, mere bluster from the palace because the king was losing his sleep over a troubling dream. Zedekiah, a king of Israel, was treated to one final sight before Nebuchadnezzar had his eyes put out—the execution of his sons, which he was forced to watch (2 Kings 25:7). And this famously tetchy king had two Jewish rebels burned alive (Jer. 29:22), a mode of execution that he would famously resurrect in the story of Daniel and his friends. Three times in the book of Daniel we read about Nebuchadnezzar's fury and rage (see Daniel 2:12; 3:13; 3:19), and when his royal highness got upset, people lost their lives. Arioch, the chief executioner, was on his way to dispatch the Hebrew Four.

Some translations describe Arioch as the chief butcher.

The second choice context that the Hebrew boys found themselves in had escalated to a second choice crisis. But faced with imminent death, Daniel and his friends refused to react.

They responded.

In the biblical story, God frequently speaks through dreams.

Jacob, a fugitive, had his famous "Jacob's ladder" dream that assured him that God was with him, would protect him and give him the land (Gen. 28:12–17). And it was as an interpreter of dreams that Joseph, sold into slavery by his treacherous brothers, rose to a place of great power in Egypt (Gen. 41:39–44), a development that, as we'll see, happened in Daniel's life too. Through a dream, Solomon, intimidated by the challenge to occupy the throne after the golden reign of his father, David, was promised wisdom, discernment, wealth, and honor (1 Kings 3:5–14).

Now, in a city infested with the occult and shrouded in confusion, violence, and immorality, the one true God was broadcasting on Nebuchadnezzar's wavelength. The outcome would be staggering. Somebody would have to step up and describe the dream and offer an interpretation. They would need discernment, and confidence. Shouldering that responsibility, facing down an already furious despot eager for blood, would have been terrifying. But first, there were two other items of critical business. Daniel would need a royal audience to ask for time, with a king who was already bent on killing his advisors because he thought they were stalling.

For time.

The second item on the agenda was even more pressing. The chief butcher was at the door, bloodied sword in hand, eager to do his work; to delay or disobey the order to dispatch Daniel and his friends would mean Arioch risked his own neck. The fate of the royal advisors made it clear: those who failed in their duties would get the chop, literally.

Someone's knocking at the door.

Somebody needs to answer it.

Who's up for it?

And so the awful gang arrived. Their torches and lanterns had announced them from a distance.

They were armed to the teeth, clutching clubs as well as swords, and ropes to bind prisoners with. And they were eager, heady because they held all the power. One of them was responsible for identifying who was to be killed. Tension crackled like electricity; perhaps there was a brief moment of silence as the arresting party paused, their torches flickering in the darkness.

It was then the one leading them broke ranks, stepped up, and kissed Jesus on the cheek, a peck of betrayal, a prearranged signal: He is the one. Seize Him.

The usual serenity of the garden of Gethsemane was suddenly shattered by pandemonium. Favored by Jesus for prayer and teaching, now a potential war breaks out as some of the mob grab Jesus. There was no light touch here, no hand on shoulder; the word used in the narrative emphasizes the physicality of the arrest.

It was then that Peter displayed a combination of bravery and stupidity. Previously he'd pledged that he would put his life on the line for Jesus (Luke 22:33), and now he made good on that promise.

Pulling a sword, he fought back, swinging wildly. It was a clumsy attempt, and he missed his target, which was helpful, because otherwise he would have been tried as a murderer.

With the best motives, Peter frantically sought to defend Jesus, but there was just one problem. He risked his life doing what Jesus didn't want, and even had to repair, because one hapless chap temporarily lost his ear in the fracas.

Why did Peter do it?

The Jews were living with the hope of a military messiah, a conquering rescuer who would set them free from the enforced exilic lockdown under the heels of the Romans. And hadn't Jesus used a metaphor of buying swords, a word picture calling them to readiness and vigilance (Luke 22:37–38), one that they'd misunderstood, which frustrated Him?

Matthew, Mark, and John describe Peter just impulsively moving into sword-swinging mode. Luke says that someone asked Jesus for a command to attack: "When Jesus' followers saw what was going to happen, they said, 'Lord, should we strike with our swords?'" (Luke 22:49).

But panicked and desperate, they did what we often do. Even if we ask God for direction, we don't wait around for a reply. Falsely secure just because the query has been made, we trust our instincts, which are notoriously unreliable.

And it's not just Peter's panicked actions that were wrong; he's infamous for clumsy, thoughtless blurting, especially when he felt squeezed into a tight spot.

The most famous example happened when Jesus began teaching His disciples that He was heading for Jerusalem, to suffering, death, and resurrection. Peter didn't like that at all, and, incredibly, took Jesus aside for a good telling off, only to receive the most stinging rebuke himself (Matt. 16:21–23). When tragedy strikes, we can feel paralyzed, immobilized by terror. But there is one part of our bodies that seems to keep on working when we're traumatized.

It's the tongue.

When the sneaker-wave of crisis suddenly breaks over us, we're caught off guard, and our immediate response is to open our mouths before engaging the brain; to scream, to yell for help, to complain, to pray. I have been more proficient in the first of these reflexes: yelling, loudly and bitterly, comes more naturally than prayer, especially when a muscle-bound murderer on a mission to still one's pulse drops by. Solomon's advice is timeless, "Do not be quick with your mouth ... let your words be few" (Eccl. 5:2). And the book of Proverbs poses the question: "Do you see someone who speaks in haste? There is more hope for a fool than for them" (Prov. 29:20).

Mark Twain observes, "A closed mouth gathers no foot."

In a crisis, we need to deliberately slow down, lest our words worsen our situation. Again, Scripture urges us to learn how to put the brake on panic-fueled verbiage:

"My dear brothers and sisters, take note of this: Everyone should be quick to listen, slow to speak and slow to become angry" (James 1:19).

Despite his youth and inexperience, Daniel turned out to be the ideal man in a crisis. Refusing panic and paralysis, he knew that cool-headed action was needed. It was time for a chat.

With the executioner.

Wisdom is generally associated with age; the assumption is that those who have walked life's road longest will be wisest, which is a false notion. I know people who are advanced in years but still navigate decisions without thought, and without care for the damage they continue to inflict. They are older but not wiser.

But for such a young man, Daniel uses measured wisdom, which must have been a challenge when you know that one wrong word could lead to one fatal strike of the sword, or worse—the death by dislocation or slow hacking we alluded to earlier.

Wisdom is not just about the gathering of information; I've met brilliant people who have made incredibly unwise decisions, shown little emotional intelligence, and systematically destroyed their closest and most vital relationships because they were clever, but foolish.

The call to live wisely is constantly repeated throughout Scripture—no less than nine chapters of the book of Proverbs summon us to choose well between what some commentators call "Lady Wisdom" and "Dame Folly."

As a life coach, I've concluded that Christians often depend more on revelation—what we think God is currently saying—than upon wisdom—what we have learned from God in our journey so far. We are truly wise when we take the insights that we've gained in the academy of life, and don't just note them, but live in the good of them, especially in times of crisis.

Facing a sharp sword, Daniel could have responded with a desperate, even pathetic cry for mercy.

A plea of innocence: we weren't even there when the king's advisors tried to pull the wool over his eyes.

How dare you, Arioch. Don't you know that we're members of the royal academy?

Wouldn't you do well to double-check that the king really wants us dead—perhaps he was just venting?

Do you want to take that risk?

A threat: do this to us, and the God we serve is going to get you.

An escape attempt. Run for your lives, boys. We're doomed anyway, so let's take our chances.

Instead, Daniel used wisdom as he talked to the executioner. And it was not just the content of his words that counted.

We're told he was tactful. The word means "tasteful." It speaks of suitability and appropriateness. Something amazing transpires, as the executioner reveals his anxiety and fear. Daniel's tone has won his trust.

In steering through our own second choice worlds, let's be diligent about our choice of words and the tone we use when under pressure, lest instead of helping dispel a crisis, we create another one.

I believe in God.

He broke into my life, unexpectedly and initially uninvited, when I was a young man, close to Daniel's age when these calamities occurred. In over four decades since, He has spoiled me, blessed me vastly beyond my expectations. There's an old hymn that encourages us to count our blessings, and name them one by one. Seriously, I've lost count.

Yet here's a solemn confession, one that shames me.

I believe there is a God who helps and cares, but then I can live and act as if heaven were empty. On Sunday I affirm the reality of His love and care, and I am absolutely sincere. But then second choices roll up, and I react as if I am simply the product of a random chemical reaction in some primeval swamp.

It's not that I'm floored by doubt, although I have my moments when I wonder. Doubt occasionally buzzes by my ears like a pesky mosquito, and I no longer fear it. Spending life to please Somebody who is currently invisible has its challenges.

But this is different. It's not believing that's the problem, but rather living in the good of that belief is more challenging. We can be theologically orthodox, but functionally atheistic.

Some of this happens because, much of the time, at least in my experience, God seems distant. His lack of proximity isn't helped by the false notion that I am on earth and He is in heaven, somewhere out there, perhaps slightly to the left of Jupiter. When I say, "Our Father, who is in heaven," I pray, which is an act of faith, but I affirm my location (here on earth) and His implied locality (up or out there in heaven). This immediately confirms a distance issue, and prayer feels like lobbing snowballs at the moon. Dallas Willard sums up the problem with customary elegance:

> Some think that God is a Wizard of Oz type being sitting in a location very remote from us. The universe is then presented to us chiefly as a vast empty space with a humanoid God and a few angels rattling around in it ... of such a "god" we can only

say good riddance. It seems that when many people
pray they do have such an image of God in their
minds. They therefore find praying psychologically
impossible or extremely difficult. No wonder.[52]

As it turns out, our translation of the so-called disciples' prayer is
misleading.

In the gospel bearing his name, Matthew uses the term "Father
in heaven" no less than twenty times. One commentator suggests that
our problem—the suggestion of a God who lives above—has been
created by a poor translation of the word "heaven," which he insists
should be the plural "heavens."

Suddenly, everything changes.

Far from suggesting that Father is distant, Jesus teaches precisely
the opposite.

The "first" heaven, biblically, is the atmosphere or air that immediately surrounds our bodies. Jesus is teaching us that God the Father
is near us and out there both. He is introducing us to the infinite,
omnipresent Father who is so very, very close, and in whom we "live
and move, and have our being" (Acts 17:28). Matthew is also giving
us a wide-screen vision of the Lord, banishing our dwarfed godlets
with the revelation that we have a Father whose authority and presence
stretches across the heavens and the earth. And this truth is far more
than abstract theology, but reaches down into our Monday morning
praying. It means that we have authority to participate in the unfolding
drama of history-making as we partner with God through our praying.

Willard adds: "The damage done to our practical faith in Christ
and in his government at hand by confusing heaven with a place

in distant or outer space or even beyond space is incalculable. Of course God is there too. But instead of heaven and God always being present with us, as Jesus shows them to be, we invariably take them to be located far away, and most likely, at a much later time—not here and not now. And should we then be surprised to feel ourselves alone?"[53]

Bad theology leads us to believe that God is, but not right here. And Nebuchadnezzar's doomed advisors believed something similar, not of God, but of their gods. Challenged by their royal boss, they responded: "No one can reveal it to the king except the gods, and they do not live among humans" (Dan. 2:11).

But Daniel knew not only that his God was present but also that God was his source, his helper. The "God of heaven" was very much entwined with matters on earth.

He later declares that in a beautiful poem of praise—the emphases are mine, but Daniel celebrates God as the everlasting giver of wisdom, knowledge, and power, the One who orders the seasons and gives authority to rulers, the revealer of what is hidden and unknown, who responds to prayers for help:

> Praise be to the name of God for ever and ever;
> wisdom and power are *his*.
> *He* changes times and seasons;
> *he* deposes kings and raises up others.
> *He* gives wisdom to the wise
> and knowledge to the discerning.
> *He* reveals deep and hidden things;
> *he* knows what lies in darkness,

and light dwells with *him*.
I thank and praise you, God of my ancestors:
You have given me wisdom and power,
you have made known to me what we asked of you,
you have made known to us the dream of the king.
(Dan. 2:20–23)

And such knowledge created humility and security in Daniel. When he ultimately stood before the king, he might have been tempted to make himself indispensable, playing up his gift and playing down God as the source of the gift. But he does the opposite, and doesn't even mention himself:

"Daniel replied, 'No wise man, enchanter, magician or diviner can explain to the king the mystery he has asked about, but there is a God in heaven who reveals mysteries. He has shown King Nebuchadnezzar what will happen in days to come'" (Dan. 2:27–28).

And again:

"The great God has shown the king what will take place in the future" (Dan. 2:45).

Knowing that God was present as source and helper meant that Daniel didn't need to fight for credit when someone else tried to steal the limelight.

Remember Arioch the executioner?

He tried to take some credit for Daniel's gift, suggesting that he had located a dream-interpreter.

The fact is that Daniel was the one who had suggested the possibility of an interpretation to Arioch. Again, this might have undermined Daniel's value to the king, which potentially could have rendered him more disposable. But when we know our source, others taking credit for what we have done might be irritating, but it doesn't really matter.

But before any of these wonders could unfold, Daniel still had a problem. He needed a temporary stay of execution, and before he could go to the king, or seek help from the King of Kings, he had a few questions for his would-be executioner.

When we find ourselves in situations likely to provoke panic and fear, investigation is better than speculation.

When chatting with an armed killer, it's a good idea to make sure that one doesn't cause upset, and as we've seen, Daniel spoke with wisdom and tact. But he also took quite a risk when he quizzed Arioch. Describing the king's edict as "harsh" created the possibility that Arioch would see this comment as treasonous. But Daniel was keen to understand the king's motivation for his actions.

When feeling threatened, get the facts.

And then face the facts.

Dr. Mark and his wife, Sarah, have spent a lifetime serving others. A brilliant plastic surgeon who spent much of his career on the mission field, he and his nurse-wife, Sarah, brought help and healing to many, specializing in rectifying birth deformities. Returning to America to the final years of practice prior to retirement, he enjoyed his hobby, flying radio-controlled aircraft and helicopters. One fateful day, he decided to replace broken rotor blades on a helicopter, not knowing that he was working with a defective part. Staring closely at the rotor to balance it, suddenly the blade sheared off and flew into his eye. He knew he was in deep trouble, and despite urgent surgery, the eye was lost—a terrible injury for anyone, potentially a disaster for a surgeon who relies on steady hands and keen eyesight. Eventually recovering, and informing his patients of his challenges, he returned to practice, fully competent—only to experience, several years later, a vitreous detachment in his other eye. He knew now that his medical career was over, and the opportunity to build a comfortable retirement lost.

A second choice experience for sure.

Sitting together in our home, I asked Mark how he handled fear, having experienced such sudden, life-altering changes.

His response surprised me, because I know the power of imagination when it comes to fear, and have watched people spend years afraid of a circumstance that never materialized. The person terrified of cancer lives a long life and dies of heart disease; the one successful in business lives in daily anxiety about financial need, but after decades of needless agitation, retires comfortably.

Mark said, "I ask the question: What is the very worst thing that can happen? And then I stare at that possibility, knowing that whatever the outcome, Jesus is with me."

Rather than rejecting the possibility of the worst, Mark interrogates the situation, and considers the outcomes. When we do that, we might be fearful, but not afraid. Nelson Mandela said: "Courage is not the absence of fear, but the triumph over it. The brave man is not he who does not feel afraid, but he who conquers that fear."[54]

With all our technology, fear continues as an untamed Goliath. In his novel *The Life of Pi*, Yann Martel writes:

> I must say a word about fear. It is life's only true opponent. Only fear can defeat life. It is a clever, treacherous adversary, how well I know. It has no decency, respects no law or convention, shows no mercy. It goes for your weakest spot, which it finds with unerring ease. It begins in your mind, always. One moment you are feeling calm, self-possessed, happy. Then fear, disguised in the garb of mild-mannered doubt, slips into your mind like a spy … The matter is difficult to put into words. For fear, real fear, such as shakes you to your foundation, such as you feel when you are brought face to face with your mortal end, nestles in your memory like a gangrene: it seeks to rot everything, even the words with which to speak of it. So you must fight hard to express it. You must fight hard to shine the light of words upon it. Because if you don't, if your fear becomes a wordless darkness that you avoid, perhaps even manage to forget, you open yourself to further attacks of fear because you never truly fought the opponent who defeated you.[55]

It's been said that we fear life. We fear death. We fear what is. We fear what is not, and we fear what might possibly be. Fear pushes us around, makes us freeze when we should flee, roughly shoves us into panic when calm reflection would be so much better. We're frightened of what we know, and terrified there are awful factors behind everyday life that we don't know. It ruins our waking, and robs us of sleep. We're afraid of intimacy, rejection, heights, and clowns. We fear failing, we fear spiders. Because of fear, nations go to war, stock markets tumble, businesses collapse. Neighbors despise the people next door, convinced that they are a menace.

Daniel faced down fear, and headed to the palace.

It's time.
Incredibly, I've been granted an audience.
That's ironic, because the man sent
to kill me has used his influence to
get me into the inner chamber.
Arioch.
He's quite the gambler.
If this goes wrong, he will lose everything because
he wasted the king's time. Sleepless and tetchy,
the king is in no mood for empty promises.
He wants answers.
I'm going to ask him for what he's
already refused to give others: time.

His throne room, impossibly opulent,

intimidates, even though I've been in

the vicinity for three long years.

I've known this man's favor. He thought we

were the best of the best, yet still he condemned

us to die with all the other advisors.

Has he changed his mind about us, about me?

Was it temper-fueled haste, or a death

sentence by careful design?

At last, I stand before him, surrounded, as always,

by guards just waiting for an order to strike.

I hope he slept last night.

I ask.

Live forever, your Majesty.

Please, I beg you, give me time, that

I might interpret your dream.

There is a long silence.

I wait for the barked command,

the strike of a sword.

He nods.

I'm dismissed.

Relief.

Joy.

Hope.

The plan worked.

There's just one further step needed.

Without it, the stay of execution will
be lifted, and my friends and I might
suffer an even more hideous death.
I need to know what the king
dreamt, and what it all means.
I need to know.

And God responded. Following his promise to the king, Daniel experiences a vision in the night, one that unlocks the mystery of Nebuchadnezzar's dream.

Once again, Daniel approaches Arioch, and persuades him to arrange yet another audience at the palace. But in the process of all this, one other component is vital: the power of praying friendship.

I thought that I'd danced in that fountain, even though there was no water in it at the time.

The popular American sitcom *Friends* focused on the interactions of six friends as they navigated life, love, careers, and challenges. The title sequence showed them dancing in what we took to be a Manhattan fountain, and the theme song spoke of promise and faithfulness.

Daniel needed God to be there for him, and help him—urgently. And so he turned, not only to friends for help, but to praying friends, a tiny community of believers who found strength and courage together. Daniel was not alone in Babylon, but was part of a praying, encouraging, supportive community.

In this episode, their Hebrew names are used.

We need to build prayerful friendships with those who know their true identities in Christ, and can pray with the authority and confidence that is theirs as a result. If we are to survive in exile and flourish when life gives us second choices, we need to be committed to deepening relationship together.

Dietrich Bonhoeffer wrote: "The physical presence of other Christians is a source of incomparable joy and strength to the believer."[56]

By the way, in researching for this book, I discovered that the fountain in Manhattan famously associated with the *Friends* series wasn't actually in Manhattan, or even in New York, but is to be found in Burbank, California, at the Warner Bros. Ranch.

The fountain was a work of fiction, as were the relationships between Chandler, Ross, Joey, Phoebe, Rachel, and Monica—the New York six. But the friendship between Daniel, Hananiah, Mishael, and Azariah, the Hebrews, was real, substantial, and prayerful.

There were no solos in Babylon, but the song of a quartet. We too need to invest in church, in friendship, in prayerful connections, because when the going gets tough in Babylon, we need others to sing along with too.

FOR REFLECTION

1. What do you think of Dr. Mark's advice to face the worst thing that could happen—to face the fear and stare it down with Jesus' help?

2. What do you fear the most?

3. Who might your praying friends be, and how might you invest in current or new relationships that will be a lifeline when second choices come?

In the second year of his reign, Nebuchadnezzar had dreams; his mind was troubled and he could not sleep.

Daniel 2:1

"Are you able to tell me what I saw in my dream and interpret it?"

Daniel replied, "No wise man, enchanter, magician or diviner can explain to the king the mystery he has asked about, but there is a God in heaven who reveals mysteries. He has shown King Nebuchadnezzar what will happen in days to come. Your dream and the visions that passed through your mind as you were lying in bed are these:

"As Your Majesty was lying there, your mind turned to things to come, and the revealer of mysteries showed you what is going to happen. As for me, this mystery has been revealed to me, not because I have greater wisdom than anyone else alive, but so that Your Majesty may know the interpretation and that you may understand what went through your mind.

"Your Majesty looked, and there before you stood a large statue—an enormous, dazzling statue, awesome in appearance. The head of the statue was made of pure gold, its chest and arms of silver, its belly and thighs of bronze, its legs of iron, its feet partly of iron and partly of baked clay. While you were watching, a rock was cut out, but not by human hands. It struck the statue on its feet of iron and clay and smashed them. Then the iron, the clay, the bronze, the silver and the gold were all broken to pieces and became like chaff on a threshing floor in the summer. The wind swept them away without leaving a trace. But the rock that struck the statue became a huge mountain and filled the whole earth.

"This was the dream, and now we will interpret it to the king. Your Majesty, you are the king of kings. The God of heaven has given you dominion and power and might and glory; in your hands he has placed all mankind and the beasts of the field and the birds in the sky. Wherever they live, he has made you ruler over them all. You are that head of gold.

"After you, another kingdom will arise, inferior to yours. Next, a third kingdom, one of bronze, will rule over the whole earth. Finally, there will be a fourth kingdom, strong as iron—for iron breaks and smashes everything—and as iron breaks things to pieces, so it will crush and break all the others. Just as you saw that the feet and toes were partly of baked clay and partly of iron, so this will be a divided kingdom; yet it will have some of the strength of iron in it, even as you saw iron mixed with clay. As the toes were partly iron and partly clay, so this kingdom will be partly strong and partly brittle. And just as you saw the iron mixed with baked clay, so the people will be a mixture and will not remain united, any more than iron mixes with clay.

"In the time of those kings, the God of heaven will set up a kingdom that will never be destroyed, nor will it be left to another people. It will crush all those kingdoms and bring them to an end, but it will itself endure forever. This is the meaning of the vision of the rock cut out of a mountain, but not by human hands—a rock that broke the iron, the bronze, the clay, the silver and the gold to pieces.

"The great God has shown the king what will take place in the future. The dream is true and its interpretation is trustworthy."

Then King Nebuchadnezzar fell prostrate before Daniel and paid him honor and ordered that an offering and incense be presented to him. The king said to Daniel, "Surely your God is the God of gods and the Lord of kings and a revealer of mysteries, for you were able to reveal this mystery."

Daniel 2:26–47

In the third year of King Belshazzar's reign, I, Daniel, had a vision, after the one that had already appeared to me.

Daniel 8:1

As I looked,
thrones were set in place, and the Ancient of Days took his seat. His clothing was as white as snow; the hair of his head was white like wool. His throne was flaming with fire, and its wheels were all ablaze. A river of fire was flowing, coming out from before him. Thousands upon thousands attended him; ten thousand times ten thousand stood before him. The court was seated, and the books were opened.

Daniel 7:9–10

7

While You Were Sleeping

It was a throwaway comment that caused quite a reaction. "It's one thing to talk to Jesus. It's another thing when Jesus talks to you," said Joy Behar, an actress and comedian, on the show *The View*. "That's called mental illness, if I'm not correct. Hearing voices."

There *is* a delusional aspect to some illnesses. But the notion of a mute God is obviously not only unbiblical, but irrational. Perhaps some would prefer that He did not have a voice, because to hear Him is to risk disruption.

God speaks in a variety of ways. Graham Tomlin wrote:

> A comment made in conversation, a sermon heard, a song in worship, a book read—God can use all of these means to speak to us, as well as when a person delivers a specific "prophecy"—insight or information given to them by the Lord—or even "a word of knowledge" (when specific details are given to somebody through the work of the Holy Spirit) or "a word of wisdom"—when someone shares supernaturally gleaned insight about what we should do. Most Christians will recall

times when a word in a sermon, a song, a word of knowledge, or a prophetic word has penetrated right down to the depths of their being. This might be called "inspired communication" which is perhaps a useful, simple definition of prophecy. When it happens it's as if you are seen through, understood, and the secrets which no one else knows are addressed and resolved by a word from someone who couldn't possibly have known what was in your heart.[57]

And now, God was once again using dreams to get His point across.

The first dream outlined above was given early in the exile period to Nebuchadnezzar. The second was given directly to Daniel. Although the dreams are sixty years apart, most believe they are parallel dreams. Both speak of four kingdoms, and then of an eternal kingdom. King Nebuchadnezzar's dream involved four sections of a statue; Daniel's featured four beasts rising up out of the sea. Both dreams feature a final fifth kingdom that will overcome all other kingdoms and be eternal.

These dreams, and the stories of Daniel as a whole, reflect six major themes:

- The unspeakable horror of human evil—we are not ascending, improving. At the heart of who we are, sin spoils.

- The announcement of God's deliverance—we are not abandoned or helpless. Help has come, and is at hand, in Christ.

- Repentance leads to deliverance—good choices change everything. Change is possible. In fact, when we meet and daily walk with God, change is not just possible, but inevitable.

- There is an invisible cosmic conflict happening—behind the scenes, warfare rages between powers of good and evil, although ultimate victory is assured. A better day is coming.

- Those who resist God and oppress His people will be judged—justice will come one day when the King of righteousness rules supreme.

- God's people, downtrodden though we are, will be victorious in the future. Our future is secure, and gloriously bright.

Throughout history, people have tried to "unlock" the book of Daniel and interpret it, sometimes attaching times and specific individuals in foolish predictions. Much of what Daniel promised came true in the period between the sixth and second centuries before Christ. What we do know for sure is that God spoke to bring hope.

Gerard Kelly calls us back to the main theme of hope in Daniel, and calls us away from foolish speculation:

"The response of the people of God to dreams and visions of this kind should not be to put on maps and calendars to plot the world's precise end, but rather to take courage in the assurance that the final scenes are already written, that the God who is sovereign over history guarantees love's victory over death. His kingdom will come and His will will be done, on earth as it is in heaven."[58]

When we find ourselves living in a second choice world, we can quickly lose hope and heart, fearing that nothing will ever change. God spoke to announce news that would stir authentic hope for Daniel and his friends. David Smith, commenting on Daniel, says,

> With Zion a smoking ruin and a bewildered and lamenting remnant living as strangers in a land with a brilliant and powerful culture which owed nothing to their faith in Yahweh, the urgent and desperate need was for a new word of comfort and renewed vision and hope.[59]

As Eugene Peterson wrote, "The prophets worked to get people who were beaten down to open themselves up to hope in God's future. In the wreckage of exile and death and humiliation and sin, the prophet ignited hope, opening lives to the new work of salvation that God is about at all times and everywhere."[60]

When we find ourselves in ongoing trying circumstances, we can forget these hopeful truths: we can change. Life can change. In

Daniel, this is not wishful thinking—it's what God communicated through those dreams.

We've already seen earlier that we don't do life in a puppet theater with God pulling the strings of every circumstance. But we must never lose sight of the fact that God's ultimate agendas, plans, and purposes will come to pass. The king of Babylon is not the ultimate ruler—the Lord is.

Scripture is God's Word to us; if someone brings a "prophecy" to us, it must be tested to see if it is in line with Scripture. It's interesting to note that Daniel's prophetic gift was actually fueled by his reading and understanding of Scripture.

As Daniel reads the prophet Jeremiah, so his heart and mind are stirred, he seeks God in prayer, which in turn leads to an appearance by the angel Gabriel.

We must have a firm foundation in Scripture. Just as the prophet Ezekiel was commanded to "eat the scroll" and then speak the word to Israel, so we in turn hear from God through Scripture.

Viv Thomas shows us how Daniel's knowledge of God kept him hopeful:

> Daniel knew that Babylon was temporary and that only his God was eternal. This sort of perspective on time has the power to reframe second choice worlds.

Daniel praised the "wisdom" of God. God is able to understand all the dimensions of people's dreams and power games. God could see under, over and through the problems presented to Daniel. The riddles and traps of this second choice world were fully known to God.

Daniel praised God for his "power." The notion is that Daniel knew God had the ability to do what he wanted to do. Daniel might be living in a second choice world but this was a world where God still operated his strength. God is as powerful in second choice worlds as he is in first.

Daniel praised God because "he changes times and seasons." God was in control of Nebuchadnezzar's time and Daniel's time. Daniel was living with the sense that God is in charge of the timing of events. He is Lord of time and the times in between time; the periods when nothing seems to be happening, when we are becalmed and it looks like there is no wind to take us forward to the destination.

Perhaps most startling is that Daniel was aware of God's ability to perceive darkness. Daniel said of God that, "he knows what lies in darkness." The darkness of Nebuchadnezzar's world was not darkness to God; to him it was as day. This is very important for people who have to live in second choice worlds. There is no darkness, riddle, mystery, relationship or task which God cannot perceive and respond to adequately. Daniel was celebrating that darkness is not total blackness to God. If that is so then there is a chance that we will be able to see what is going on and grasp how to handle our second choice worlds with all of their inevitable darkness and confusion.[61]

The interpretation of Nebuchadnezzar's dream was a preparatory education to Daniel—he learned how to hear God. By gradual steps, each revelation preparing him for the succeeding one, God developed Daniel's prophetic gift.

- In the second and fourth chapters he is just an interpreter of Nebuchadnezzar's dreams.
- Then he has a dream himself, but it is only a vision in a dream of the night (Dan. 7:1–2).
- Then follows a vision in a waking state (Dan. 8:1–14).
- Lastly, in the two final revelations, the ecstatic state is no longer needed (Dan. 9:20).

Hearing from God is a learned art. But it usually involves enrolling in the academy of confusion and, at times, bewilderment.

I was frustrated and angry, and I slammed the front door hard behind
me, a noisy amen to what I felt had been an exasperating evening.
Meeting for a Bible study in a home was the setting for the resulting
angst; we had spent an hour or so chatting about the supernatural.
Two of our number had just come back from overseas travel, where
they had apparently witnessed some impressive miracles of healing.
We had talked about the need for us to see more genuine Holy Spirit
activity where we live. I should have been inspired, but was irritated
instead. I'm sure that it's wonderful for the Chinese church to be
raising the dead, particularly if you're Chinese and you happened to
be around to see the corpse involved suddenly perk up, but it's not
such fun at a distance.

Frankly, being treated to a diet of distant stories about God working overtime elsewhere, or in the past, is a bit like being starving and
homeless, and peering longingly through the bushes at a royal garden
party. You might start off merely salivating, but after a while you get
a bit outraged at your own lack of cucumber sandwiches. Hence my
door-slamming routine. How come, I raged, God couldn't show up a
bit more around here? Yes, I know all the but-we-live-in-a-culture-of-
unbelief apologetics routines, but why couldn't God help us clear the
aforementioned cultural fog, with a few faith-building activities that
might get our eyes popping and our hearts quickened? As I slammed
the front door, I think I closed a door in my own heart as well. I
decided that talk of miracles was tiring, and felt the need to bolt and
double lock myself off from prophecies that aren't terribly prophetic.
I had been in enough charismatic meetings where "words of knowledge" were given that were less than exciting, and where apparently
meaningless revelations were greeted with way too much enthusiasm.

The next morning I awoke with the rasping throat and foggy head of a heavy cold. Wondering if perhaps I might have been smitten by this plague as a judgment for my stroppiness, I decided (having turned my back on healing for good) to request it just one more time.

I prayed.

The rasping throat remained.

That night I went to bed armed with a Vicks inhaler for each nostril, two boxes of Kleenex, and a drip feed of Night Nurse.

The door of my heart, as it were, was slammed, locked, bolted, and I was thinking of nailing it up permanently.

But while most of the time God waits to be wanted, there are occasions when He will come as a loving burglar, scaling our pathetic defensive walls and flicking off our security systems, over-riding them with what at first seems to be unwelcome love.

The Fatherly intruder came while I slept; perhaps the only time my mind and mouth are still enough to allow Him a word in edge-ways. I dreamed the same, strange dream over and over: and even as I share it with you, I feel like I am broadcasting from the charismatic twilight zone.

Bear with me if you can. In the dream, I was standing on a railway station: Pemberton Station. A railway official stood on the platform and chatted with me while I waited for a train that never actually came. His chat filled me in on all kinds of information about this place called Pemberton. When I awoke, the dream had not evaporated like the morning dew (as most of my dreams do). It was crystal clear, vivid and sharp in my memory. And as I lay there in the warm coma that is called waking up, it occurred to me that I would bump into someone called Pemberton that very day, and that I would tell them what the railway porter had told me, and that it would speak to them of hope, and of better days ahead.

This was unusual, strange, and would take a major bit of acrobatic organization from God to make such a thing happen. Especially as I had never met anyone called Pemberton before.

I was due to speak at "Equipped to Lead," a day of leadership training that would be attended by around sixty people: not exactly a cast of thousands from which to pick a Pemberton. I drove excitedly to the hall where we were due to gather, rushed in, and grabbed the list of pre-registered delegates. My featherlight heart turned to lead as I scanned the list and my eyes hurried down in search of *P* for *Pemberton*. There were none present. It was like a bad taste in my mouth, yet another disappointment to compound my feeling that locked doors were good doors. If faith were a vital sign, I would have been pronounced dead at that moment.

Just before the first session was due to begin, a breathless couple rushed up to the registration table, and announced that they wanted to join the course, but hadn't had a chance to pre-register. Would it be okay? I smiled my agreement, asked for their names, and almost fell over. They were Mr. and Mrs. Pemberton. I think I said something giftedly stupid like "Nice to meet you. I was on your station all last night," but then asked if I could talk to them in the break. I couldn't believe it. Suddenly belief was believable again.

I got to tell them my railway dream, which they said made good sense, but I asked them to think on it, share it with whoever they wanted to (I do believe in personal prophecy, but not private prophecy). We laughed and cried some together and they telephoned me a few weeks later to say, yes, they had thought, prayed, and shared the word I gave them with trusted friends, and did feel that God had clearly spoken.

When I was worn out and faithless, ready to jump the charismatic ship for good and wave goodbye to the gifts of the Holy Spirit, God picked my lock, and my brain ... and beautifully broke through my little defense system.

And this is where I was tempted to end this part of this chapter, with that true and hopefully inspiring story about the God who speaks through dreams. But there is a glaring issue here. This episode in Daniel ends with the remarkable sight of the most powerful man in the world prostrating himself before a foreign exile; a worshipper of gods acknowledging the might of the one true God.

Marvelous indeed. Incredible.

But the challenge is simple: If God could speak to the king, unravel the riddle in a night vision to Daniel, bringing his highness low, literally ...

... then why did God not nudge the king to at least repatriate Daniel and his friends, allowing them to return home from exile for a wondrous reunion with family and friends?

Perhaps there are answers in this specific situation.

We've already seen that the nation of Israel was under judgment, and the Hebrew Four were caught up in that. God obviously had a strategic plan in Babylon, one in which Daniel played a vital part.

But surely Daniel might have been tempted to wonder, even as he poured out praise and thanksgiving, why does God respond to some requests with an instant, overnight answer, while others seem to go unheeded?

Much has been written and spoken about the problem of unanswered prayer. Pete Greig has written an outstanding book on the subject, with the telling title, *God on Mute*. He also found that, while unanswered prayer creates issues, answered prayer can be troubling too.

He and his wife, Sammy, were on their honeymoon, and decided to see the harrowing movie *Schindler's List*. Returning to their cottage and realizing that their car was about to run out of petrol, Pete prayed that God would get them home. Thankful when they made it safely, it occurred to him that there was a problem with the idea that God had helped them.

> The madness of it all suddenly struck me. How on earth can I believe God did that, that He got us home safely without running out of petrol, just to save me the inconvenience of walking a few miles with a petrol can?
>
> "Erm, because He loves us?" Sammy ventured warily, bringing me back to the simple stuff as she always does.
>
> "Yes, of course," I snapped. "So why didn't He love those people in that concentration camp crying out to Him for help? I mean, do we seriously,

honestly believe that God heard my prayer for petrol in Ambleside yet ignored their prayers in Auschwitz?"

"Darling, it's our honeymoon," Sammy reminded me. "This really isn't a great time for a crisis of faith." And then a mischievous grin flashed across her face. "Pass me the car keys."

"What for?"

"If it helps you cheer up, let's keep driving until the car breaks down. You'll lose your dignity and walk for miles but at least you'll keep your faith."

Schindler's List isn't a great film to watch on your honeymoon.[62]

Do we want God to be involved in the details of our lives? Surely, we respond with a resounding "Yes."

Do we understand why life can seem littered with trivial blessings when much greater problems scream for a solution?

No.

The God who was described by Daniel as the "revealer of mysteries" doesn't resolve every mystery. Faith is not just about what we know, but trusting in what we don't know. Unless we acknowledge that tension, we will never stand firm when second choices threaten to unsettle us.

I stand before him, afraid to look up.

Everything hinges on this moment.

Life or death.

He is curt with his question.

"Are you able to tell me what I saw

in my dream and interpret it?"

It's not a trick question, but I

pause before replying.

I think I have the key to unlock his dream.

But if I'm right, God is the One

who put that key in my hand.

I need to explain.

I can help, O King, but only

because God has helped me.

It's not that I'm wiser than the rest.

It's God.

And so I tell him.

His eyes widen, first with amazement,

and then raw fear.

Now he knows that the God of heaven knows

him, is speaking to him, calling him.

And then it happens.

He rises from his throne, and

does the unthinkable.

He throws himself down before me.

Me.

Minutes ago I was still under

sentence of death, and now …

the king is on the floor, crying out words

about the One, True, Real God.

My God.

Amazing. Incredible. Stunning.

Now, surely, everything is going to be

different, for my people who are trapped

here in Babylon, for my friends, for me.

Not so.

FOR REFLECTION

1. Daniel received prophetic insight for Nebuchadnezzar. Have you ever sensed that God gave you wisdom or insight to share with another individual? What happened?

2. Have you experienced God's guidance when making an important decision? How?

3. Is there a "mystery" about life and faith that you particularly struggle with?

King Nebuchadnezzar made an image of gold, sixty cubits high and six cubits wide, and set it up on the plain of Dura in the province of Babylon. He then summoned the satraps, prefects, governors, advisers, treasurers, judges, magistrates and all the other provincial officials to come to the dedication of the image he had set up. So the satraps, prefects, governors, advisers, treasurers, judges, magistrates and all the other provincial officials assembled for the dedication of the image that King Nebuchadnezzar had set up, and they stood before it.

Then the herald loudly proclaimed, "Nations and peoples of every language, this is what you are commanded to do: As soon as you hear the sound of the horn, flute, zither, lyre, harp, pipe and all kinds of music, you must fall down and worship the image of gold that King Nebuchadnezzar has set up. Whoever does not fall down and worship will immediately be thrown into a blazing furnace."

Therefore, as soon as they heard the sound of the horn, flute, zither, lyre, harp and all kinds of music, all the nations and peoples of every language fell down and worshiped the image of gold that King Nebuchadnezzar had set up.

At this time some astrologers came forward and denounced the Jews. They said to King Nebuchadnezzar, "May the king live forever! Your Majesty has issued a decree that everyone who hears the sound of the horn, flute, zither, lyre, harp, pipe and all kinds of music must fall down and worship the image of gold, and that whoever does not fall down and worship will be thrown into a blazing furnace. But there are some Jews whom you have set over the affairs of the province of Babylon—Shadrach, Meshach and Abednego—who pay no attention to you, Your Majesty. They neither serve your gods nor worship the image of gold you have set up."

Furious with rage, Nebuchadnezzar summoned Shadrach, Meshach and Abednego. So these men were brought before the king, and Nebuchadnezzar said to them, "Is it true, Shadrach, Meshach and Abednego, that you do not serve my god or worship the image of gold I have set up? Now when you hear the sound of the horn, flute, zither, lyre, harp, pipe and all kinds of music, if you are ready to fall down and worship the image I made, very good. But if you do not worship it, you will be thrown immediately into a blazing furnace. Then what god will be able to rescue you from my hand?"

Shadrach, Meshach and Abednego replied to him, "King Nebuchadnezzar, we do not need to defend ourselves before you in this matter. If we are thrown into the blazing furnace, the God we serve is able to deliver us from it, and he will deliver us from Your Majesty's hand. But even if he does not, we want you to know, Your Majesty, that we will not serve your gods or worship the image of gold you have set up."

Then Nebuchadnezzar was furious with Shadrach, Meshach and Abednego, and his attitude toward them changed. He ordered the furnace heated seven times hotter than usual and commanded some of the strongest soldiers in his army to tie up Shadrach, Meshach and Abednego and throw them into the blazing furnace. So these men, wearing their robes, trousers, turbans and other clothes, were bound and thrown into the blazing furnace. The king's command was so urgent and the furnace so hot that the flames of the fire killed the soldiers who took up Shadrach, Meshach and Abednego, and these three men, firmly tied, fell into the blazing furnace.

Then King Nebuchadnezzar leaped to his feet in amazement and asked his advisers, "Weren't there three men that we tied up and threw into the fire?"

They replied, "Certainly, Your Majesty." He said, "Look! I see four men walking around in the fire, unbound and unharmed, and the fourth looks like a son of the gods."

Nebuchadnezzar then approached the opening of the blazing furnace and shouted, "Shadrach, Meshach and Abednego, servants of the Most High God, come out! Come here!"

So Shadrach, Meshach and Abednego came out of the fire, and the satraps, prefects, governors and royal advisers crowded around them. They saw that the fire had not harmed their bodies, nor was a hair of their heads singed; their robes were not scorched, and there was no smell of fire on them.

Then Nebuchadnezzar said, "Praise be to the God of Shadrach, Meshach and Abednego, who has sent his angel and rescued his servants! They trusted in him and defied the king's command and were willing to give up their lives rather than serve or worship any god except their own God. Therefore I decree that the people of any nation or language who say anything against the God of Shadrach, Meshach and Abednego be cut into pieces and their houses be turned into piles of rubble, for no other god can save in this way." Then the king promoted Shadrach, Meshach and Abednego in the province of Babylon.

Daniel 3:1–30

8

Crazy Faith

As the plane taxied down the runway, engines humming ready for takeoff, I broke into a cold sweat, and it was not because of a fear of flying. After five years of living in the USA, we were heading back to England. Sensing a clear call to be part of a church in the south of England, we were excited—and scared. Finances were scarce. The church had kindly offered to contribute £4,000 toward our annual income, but with interest rates at over 16 percent (a modest house would demand an annual mortgage of £10,000), there was a huge gap. I made my living as an itinerant Bible teacher, but I had no idea if invitations would be forthcoming in the UK. We had an apartment rented from a couple in the church, but it was only for six months while they served in a mission project overseas. After that, we would have to find a more permanent home.

We had taken faith steps before, stepping away from a salary nearly four years earlier, our income coming exclusively from my itinerant travels in the USA. But back then, American churches, many of them with large budgets, were able to be more generous than those in the UK.

We had sent three crates of belongings ahead, and had a small savings account, but one that would only pay for our living costs for a month or so.

Hence the sweat. What would become of us?

God helped. Opportunities opened. We met a kindly bank manager who agreed to give us a mortgage despite our meager and uncertain income—a gracious step that would never be allowed these days.

But as I reflect on what happened back then, three decades ago, I'm asking myself some tough questions: If God asked me to take a radical, seemingly crazy step of faith now, would I be able to do it? Would I stay true to the vows of faithfulness that I offered to God in my youth? To frame a question that I touched on earlier, having given my life to Jesus, have I gradually taken it back again?

Around nineteen years have passed since King Nebuchadnezzar bowed humbly before Daniel and acknowledged the true and only God, but now things have gone seriously downhill.

Nebuchadnezzar has made a stunning image of gold, ninety feet high and nine feet wide. A victorious warrior, he has just returned from finishing the Jewish and Syrian wars. Nebuchadnezzar's earlier dream made an impact at the time, but it has not made him a committed follower of the one true God. What we did, gave, and prayed yesterday does not mean that we are committed to Christ today.

Daniel is nowhere to be seen in this episode; probably he was away in some distant place, engaged in some diplomatic matters. There had not been time for the general summons (Dan. 3:2) to reach him, before the dedication. And perhaps the Jews' enemies found it more politically prudent to begin by attacking Shadrach, Meshach, and Abednego, who were easy targets. Daniel could wait. His time would come.

In a way, Nebuchadnezzar's idolatry shouldn't shock us too much. Ancient idolaters thought each nation had its own gods, and, in addition to these, foreign gods might be worshipped. The Jewish religion was the only exclusive one that claimed all homage for Jehovah as the only true God.

The pressure on the Hebrew Three was intense. Death by fire was a common mode of punishment in Babylon. This is not a children's story.

The awful furnace stood ready—commentators usually assume it was cast in metal and beehive-shaped, with an opening on the top into which the men were thrown, and a door at the side through which the horrors inside could be viewed. The drama is heightened by the detailed description of the heat of the furnace, which was blazing, heated seven times hotter than usual, and so hot that soldiers guarding the three were killed. This was a fiery trial, quite literally. But the three lads stood firm in faith.

Crazy faith, yet decidedly resolute and calm, considering the circumstances.

This firing up of the furnace was a demand to worship the state. We'd do well to understand there is a huge difference between patriotism—a love and appreciation for the country, the community in which we live, a good thing—and nationalism—the notion that our nation stands above others—an evil idea. Some Christians mingle their faith with their political views, almost assigning messianic status to the candidate of choice, who can do no wrong. Those who have opposing views are considered to be less than Christian.

When we succumb to the seduction of nationalism, political preferences soon transcend our Christian values. The kingdom of God is swapped for a political idea, and concern for community is turned into relentless self-interest—what works best for me. Nationalism is idolizing the state. Jesus is no longer the answer; our politicians are. Love is exchanged for fear, anger, and self-preservation. In the clamor and the ranting, Christians are no longer distinguishable from the baying crowd; in fact, they contribute to the noise, Bibles in hand.

Commenting on this episode in Daniel, John Lennox observes: "It's an all too familiar scenario as history repeatedly testifies, the attempt to harness religion in the interest of the … state, by making the state an object of worship."[63]

We are called to bow down, not to a nation, or a human personality, but to Christ alone. There is only one Messiah.

Faith can have a "reckless" quality. Viv Thomas comments:

> Certainly there was something reckless about
> the way these three Hebrews behaved before
> Nebuchadnezzar's authoritative image; it depended
> on their sense that they were in the palm of God's
> hand and that he was the one who would dispose
> of their lives as he saw fit. It was that recklessness
> which opened the community to their message.
> Their stance against the forces of the culture were
> the initial tremors which brought the lord of the
> culture to his knees and Babylon face to face with
> the Hebrews' God.
>
> Living in this inattentive way brings great
> power; we are able to live freely and to great effect.
> In our first choice—and often self-centered—world
> we hold onto the consequences. The big questions
> are "What will I get out of this?," and "Will it do
> me good?" We drive ourselves into ourselves and
> begin to live narrowly. We are cramped within
> a small and restrictive space of self; our primary
> characteristic is constriction. This explains why so
> many Christians appear to live such weird lives. On
> the one hand they have a huge God, they live in
> a world of earth-shattering concepts; and yet they
> live tight little lives which have no more than an
> occasional fleeting reference to the God they know.

If we proclaim that God owns the world, its past, present and future, but cannot live with some sense of abandon and freedom which follows on from this claim, then we start to live in a split world, the world—to be frank—of hypocrisy, and it eventually shows.

We are so strongly gripped by self-protection, security and success that we often fail to see that God occasionally leads us into second choice worlds primarily for the sake of others. One mark of God's omnipotence is his ability to do more than one thing at once, and he often demonstrates this in our lives. It is true that he leads us through tough situations for our own sakes but the core of some of our difficulties is that he leads us through second choice worlds for others. Through the plagues of Egypt God set his people free but also explained himself to the Egyptians. Isaac was near to sacrificial death and it was Abraham to whom God spoke, not Isaac.

When Meshach, Shadrach and Abednego were facing death it was all to do with Babylon, their second choice world. Being able to live through our second choice world often requires us to grasp that we are not the point of it; someone or something else is. This is hard work for many of us because we have been brought up in a self-dominated world, but this defect does not entitle us to avoid this work if we want to truly engage our worlds of second choice. In times of difficulty over-attention to ourselves gets in the way of engaging with God's purpose for us.[64]

Perhaps this seems like a scenario that we will never face. But our recklessness can be expressed in many small choices that add up, choices that say that we will not participate in the thinking and practices of the empire, the culture around us. As we quietly refuse binge drinking, as we determine to choose purity, as we consider our buying choices where much of what we consume is created in dangerous sweatshops, we refuse to bow the knee when the band strikes up and the music plays. When we choose what's right, however graciously, people will frown and even rage, because our gentle refusal implies that something is wrong with the prevailing view. There might be further costs. When we refuse to lie to get the sale, when we determine not to cook the books when the boss stands over us, we might lose our jobs. Who knows? In the future, we might lose our freedom. Our lives. The followers of Jesus say this in response: Whatever the outcome, so be it.

The unwavering response of the young Hebrews was remarkable. Respectful, but very firm, they refused to bow the knee, and they also refused to apologize for their action, realizing that the king could snuff out their lives with one barked command.

They confessed their allegiance to the true God, and testified to God's power. "Our God is able to deliver us from the furnace of blazing fire." The Hebrew text here conveys the strongest possible assurance. The thought might be paraphrased: "He is infinitely able to rescue us."

But it is then that they make one of the most remarkable statements to be found in the Bible:

> If we are thrown into the blazing furnace, the God
> we serve is able to deliver us from it, and he will
> deliver us from Your Majesty's hand. But even if
> he does not, we want you to know, Your Majesty,
> that we will not serve your gods or worship the
> image of gold you have set up. (Dan. 3:17–18)

Some Christians are quick to criticize when others pray a prayer that includes the caveat, "If it be Thy will." That's lack of faith, they sniff. We should be bolder. But that's what the Hebrew lads prayed, submitting themselves to whatever God decided. And that's the prayer that Jesus prayed in Gethsemane, surely the place where faith and faithfulness shone so brightly.

The faith of these three youths was unconditional. Theirs was not a *quid pro quo* relationship with God. This statement inspires us when life becomes a trial, and God seems distant. We are called to "though" faith and not "if" faith. Pastor George Ross stated:

> I have served in the ministry 31 years and I have
> come to understand that there are two kinds of

faith. One says, "if everything goes well, if my life is prosperous, if I'm happy, if nobody I love dies, if I'm successful, then I will believe in God, say my prayers, go to church and give what I can afford." The other says "though the cause of evil prosper, though I sweat in Gethsemane, though I must drink my cup at Calvary, nevertheless, precisely then I will trust the Lord who made me." So Job cries, "Though he slay me yet but I trust him."

The determined statement of the Hebrew Three can also help us when we are praying for healing: God is able, but even if He does not answer us in the way we want Him to, we will not surrender or bow the knee to doubt or complacency. And failure to pray this way, and placing false expectations on those who are not healed, can damage those who suffer.

Philip Yancey, in his book *Where Is God When It Hurts?*, details the story of a nationally celebrated track star, Brian Sternberg, a record-holding pole-vaulter.[65] At just nineteen years of age, he set his first world record. Banner headlines celebrated his incredible success—and then, in 1963, Brian's world changed in a moment. Breaking his neck in a trampolining accident, Brian was paralyzed and wheelchair-bound, his sporting career obviously snuffed out. Less than a year after the accident, writing for a magazine, Brian made this powerful statement, which is not unlike the determined response that the Hebrew Three gave: "Having faith is a necessary step toward one of two things. Being healed is one of them. Peace of mind, if healing does not come, is the other. Either one will suffice."

But visiting Brian a decade after the accident, Yancey discovered that Brian had lost that sense of peace, because some well-meaning Christians had told him that if he would just have enough faith, he could stand up and walk away from his wheelchair.

In Brian's mind, faith now meant that there remained not two options for God, but only one, and that was complete healing. Only complete healing would suffice. He was putting his faith in faith. Some were amazed at the great faith of this young man who still said God would heal him. Others said he lacked faith, or he would already be healed. Yet the fact remained that when Philip Yancey left the house of Brian Sternberg, he sensed the mood of "an uncompleted, uncomfortable struggle mixed with tough, undying faith. As Brian struggled to find enough human faith, he forgot that God is sovereign, and he lost his peace of mind."[66]

True faith trusts God, whatever the outcome—and that statement is so easy to write and vaguely believe, but so difficult to live when pain is intense.

Gordon Temple, who for years led a charity that works hard for inclusion of the blind, offers wise advice, and points us to some heroes of faith who often go uncelebrated:

> How is it possible, we often ask ourselves, to come to God for healing and genuine faith, yet with the

awareness that healing may not come? How do we manage the false expectations of well-meaning Christian friends whose own faith insists that we really ought to be healed by now? For those with a long-term illness and disability, to ask God for healing is to put their faith, and the faith of others, on the line. The three friends who faced the furnace had faith—but they faced up to the possibility that the outcome of their faith might not be the outcome they had wished for or "believed" for. This strength came from the realization that the outcome was not going to change anything: either the standing of God in their eyes or the trust they were determined to place in Him. With this assurance they walked resolutely into the situation—and God showed his power. Disabled believers walk this tightrope time after time; trusting God for healing, and yet knowing, if no healing comes, that he is still God—and still worthy of their lifelong trust. And for those of us who have not yet experienced disability, let's not make the mistake of seeing disabled people as one-dimensional—defined only by their disability—with their only conceivable need being for healing. Instead, let's share the journey of faith as they, as with all of us, face the multidimensional challenges of life for which an unshakable trust in God is the key to real victory.[67]

The Hebrew Three, wearing their instantly combustible robes, trousers, turbans, and other clothes, were bound and thrown into the blazing furnace. The heat kills the soldiers responsible for throwing them in.

And now there are four men in the fire. God was in there with them, and the only thing burned up is the rope.

We are not promised that we will evade pressure and pain. We are promised eternal, everlasting presence: God with us. In Christ, whatever comes, we will never be alone again.

Not only do they emerge from the fire, but they were not "burned" in their character by the ordeal. Pressure can create perfume, as much persecuted Romanian pastor Richard Wurmbrand wrote: "As in the book of Daniel, when the three young men who were put in the furnace did not smell like the fire upon being delivered from it, so the Christians who have been in Communist prisons don't smell like bitterness against the Communists. A flower, if you bruise it under your feet, rewards you by giving you his perfume. Likewise Christians tortured by the Communists reward their torturers by love."[68]

Anna Lee Stangl visits Christian prisoners in Peru and has found the same "perfume" there:

> I have seen a light and a hope radiating from the inside the dark, damp prison cells of Peru that I have rarely seen in a "free" church. I have been the recipient of immense Christian generosity and hospitality from prisoners who invited me to eat the precious food their impoverished family brought

for them on their weekly visit. I have heard the true
sound of joy in the singing voices of Christians
who have no rational reason to be joyful. I have
heard words of hope uttered in an impossible
situation that convicted me of my own puny faith.
Paradoxically, it is by going into these prisons that
I am reminded what freedom really is.[69]

This has always been the case throughout Christian history:
pressure created perfume.

Tertullian, a chronicler of the sufferings of the early church,
wrote: "Your cruelty against us does not profit you, however exquisite. Instead it tempts people to our sect. As often as you do us down,
the more we grow in number. The very obstinacy you criticize teaches
for us. For who on seeing it is not excited to enquire what lies behind
it? Who, having enquired, does not embrace our faith?"[70]

Before we move on, let's remember that persecution is not just
what happened in history.

It's easy to think that everyone lives as we do. Rather than considering statistics, the true story of Esther is a sobering reminder of
what believers face. Esther is from Nigeria, and was just seventeen
years old when she became a prisoner of the Boko Haram group.

When the first gunshots rang out, Esther was at home with her
ailing father. As terrified screams pierced the air, Esther and her

father hurried to escape. But it was too late. They were surrounded by their attackers. The men showed no mercy to Esther's father, striking him down and leaving him in a heap on the ground. Esther was carried off, all the while looking back to see if her father would rise. But he did not. Esther would not see her father again.

Life in the hands of the Boko Haram terrorists became the worst nightmare Esther could ever imagine. They tried everything to get Esther and the other girls they had kidnapped to renounce Christ. The men also violated the girls repeatedly. "I cannot count how many men raped me. Every time they came back from their attacks, they would rape us ... defile us ..." Esther shares before turning silent. It will take her a moment to regain control of her emotions.

"Each passing day, I hated myself more and more. I felt that God had forsaken me," Esther says. "There were times I was angry with God ... but still I could not renounce Him. I found myself remembering His promise to never leave me."

After a while, Esther discovered she was pregnant. Then, about a year after she was kidnapped, God intervened and used the military to rescue Esther and the other women. Back in her village, the joy of her freedom did not last. Many people were not eager to welcome back the "Boko Haram women."

"They mocked me because I was pregnant," Esther remembers. "What broke my heart even more was that they refused to call my daughter 'Rebecca.' They referred to her as 'Boko.'"

Through her church, Esther was connected to Open Doors. She attended a trauma care seminar, where she was able to release her pain and anguish at the foot of a hand-carved cross.

"When I pinned that piece of paper to the cross, it felt like I was handing all my sorrow over to God. It felt light within me. When the trainer later removed all the pieces of paper from the cross and burnt it to ashes, I felt like all my sorrow and shame disappeared, never to come back again."

She also received food and other practical help. She shares, "I have no family other than Open Doors. After hearing my story, you did not despise me but encouraged me and showed me love. Thank you so much!"

As we realize that many of our brothers and sisters suffer daily pressure and persecution, let's pray, give to agencies that coordinate support for the persecuted, write to those who can influence, that they might speak out in the corridors of power on behalf of those who have no voice of their own. We can also write letters to those persecuted, assuring them of our prayers and support.

When we refuse to bow the knee, miracles can happen. As we'll see, the king sent out a letter—circulated around the earth—speaking of what the true God had done. Three men said no, and said yes to God, and the world felt the reverberations. As millions of Jesus followers choose well each day, we are the light, the salt, the beacon people that God has always wanted in this world. How do you change the world? Live faithfully as a citizen and agent of the kingdom where the one true King lives and reigns.

You catch my eye
In the eye of the storm;
You hold the ointment appointments
When hell's hornets swarm.
When I find no time for stillness
You tell me there's still time;
When my words are clashing symbols,
You are Reason
Rhythm
Rhyme.

You are the unexpected cheer that lifts my game;
In the vinegar and lemon juice of life
You are champagne.

You are a bed of roses
On a crowded street;
A peppermint balm
To my blistered feet:
You are rich in rest,
When rest is radium-rare.
By cool pools you position me
With passion you petition me;

In fog and smog,
You recondition my air.

You are the song that rises in my soul;
The coin that clatters in my begging bowl.

Like a goat's milk bath
To Cleopatra;
Like honey on the throat
To Frank Sinatra:
You surround me to astound me, you sooth and
      smooth.

You are the stalker who is good for me;
The jailer who can set me free;
The trap and snare to bind me
Into love.

You who have refined me,
Come find me;
Mind me;
By the grace grind me:
Bind me, gentle jailer,
Into love.[71]

Gerard Kelly

FOR REFLECTION

1. How is your faith different from what it was when you began your journey as a Christian?

2. Can you think of an example from your own life when faith seemed "reckless"?

3. How does "pressure birth perfume"?

King Nebuchadnezzar,

To the nations and peoples of every language, who live in all the earth: May you prosper greatly! It is my pleasure to tell you about the miraculous signs and wonders that the Most High God has performed for me.

How great are his signs, how mighty his wonders! His kingdom is an eternal kingdom; his dominion endures from generation to generation. I, Nebuchadnezzar, was at home in my palace, contented and prosperous. I had a dream that made me afraid. As I was lying in bed, the images and visions that passed through my mind terrified me. So I commanded that all the wise men of Babylon be brought before me to interpret the dream for me. When the magicians, enchanters, astrologers and diviners came, I told them the dream, but they could not interpret it for me. Finally, Daniel came into my presence and I told him the dream. (He is called Belteshazzar, after the name of my god, and the spirit of the holy gods is in him.)

Daniel 4:1–8

Twelve months later, as the king was walking on the roof of the royal palace of Babylon, he said, "Is not this the great Babylon I have built as the royal residence, by my mighty power and for the glory of my majesty?"

Even as the words were on his lips, a voice came from heaven, "This is what is decreed for you, King Nebuchadnezzar: Your royal authority has been taken from you. You will be driven away from people and will live with the wild animals; you will eat grass like the ox. Seven times will pass by for you until you acknowledge that the Most High is sovereign over all kingdoms on earth and gives them to anyone he wishes."

Immediately what had been said about Nebuchadnezzar was fulfilled. He was driven away from people and ate grass like the ox. His body was drenched with the dew of heaven until his hair grew like the feathers of an eagle and his nails like the claws of a bird.

At the end of that time, I, Nebuchadnezzar, raised my eyes toward heaven, and my sanity was restored. Then I praised the Most High; I honored and glorified him who lives forever.

His dominion is an eternal dominion; his kingdom endures from generation to generation. All the peoples of the earth are regarded as nothing. He does as he pleases with the powers of heaven and the peoples of the earth. No one can hold back his hand or say to him: "What have you done?"

At the same time that my sanity was restored, my honor and splendor were returned to me for the glory of my kingdom. My advisers and nobles sought me out, and I was restored to my throne and became even greater than before. Now I, Nebuchadnezzar, praise and exalt and glorify the King of heaven, because everything he does is right and all his ways are just. And those who walk in pride he is able to humble.

Daniel 4:29–37

King Belshazzar gave a great banquet for a thousand of his nobles and drank wine with them. While Belshazzar was drinking his wine, he gave orders to bring in the gold and silver goblets that Nebuchadnezzar his father had taken from the temple in Jerusalem, so that the king and his nobles, his wives and his concubines might drink from them. So they brought in the gold goblets that had been taken from the temple of God in Jerusalem, and the king and his nobles, his wives and his concubines drank from them. As they drank the wine, they praised the gods of gold and silver, of bronze, iron, wood and stone.

Suddenly the fingers of a human hand appeared and wrote on the plaster of the wall, near the lampstand in the royal palace. The king watched the hand as it wrote. His face turned pale and he was so frightened that his legs became weak and his knees were knocking.

Daniel 5:1–6

Then Daniel answered the king, "You may keep your gifts for yourself and give your rewards to someone else. Nevertheless, I will read the writing for the king and tell him what it means.

"Your Majesty, the Most High God gave your father Nebuchadnezzar sovereignty and greatness and glory and splendor. Because of the high position he gave him, all the nations and peoples of every language dreaded and feared him. Those the king wanted to put to death, he put to death; those he wanted to spare, he spared; those he wanted to promote, he promoted; and those he wanted to humble, he humbled. But when his heart became arrogant and hardened with pride, he was deposed from his royal throne and stripped of his glory. He was driven away from people and given the mind of an animal; he lived with the wild donkeys and ate grass like the ox; and his body was drenched with the dew of heaven, until he acknowledged that the Most High God is sovereign over all kingdoms on earth and sets over them anyone he wishes.

"But you, Belshazzar, his son, have not humbled yourself, though you knew all this. Instead, you have set yourself up against the Lord of heaven. You had the goblets from his temple brought to you, and you and your nobles, your wives and your concubines drank wine from them. You praised the gods of silver and gold, of bronze, iron, wood and stone, which cannot see or hear or understand. But you did not honor the God who holds in his hand your life and all your ways. Therefore he sent the hand that wrote the inscription.

"This is the inscription that was written:

MENE, MENE, TEKEL, PARSIN

"Here is what these words mean:

Mene: God has numbered the days of
your reign and brought it to an end.

Tekel: You have been weighed on the
scales and found wanting.

Peres: Your kingdom is divided and given
to the Medes and Persians."

Then at Belshazzar's command, Daniel was clothed in
purple, a gold chain was placed around his neck, and he
was proclaimed the third highest ruler in the kingdom.

That very night Belshazzar, king of the Babylonians,
was slain, and Darius the Mede took over
the kingdom, at the age of sixty-two.

Daniel 5:17–31

9

The Writing's on the Wall

He had a difficult childhood. The son of a Syrian, born and brought up in the US, he'd been given up for adoption, and described his birth parents simply as "my sperm and egg bank." By the age of two, he was so difficult to handle, his adoptive parents considered returning him to care. As a young child, he had a reputation as a brilliant little terror, often playing pranks that landed him in trouble. As a student, he sometimes relied on charity, going to the local Buddhist temple for food handouts. Some tagged him as an arrogant bully. One of his companions said that he knew that he was the cleverest in the room, and wanted everyone around him to know it. Keen on seeking spiritual enlightenment, he embarked on lengthy monastic retreats. Eccentric, he's been described as an odd individual who would greet his clients "with his underwear hanging out, barefoot."

People in his service avoided meeting him in the halls of his palace, fearing that they would lose everything if they encountered him. He chose to wear a uniform of black, which probably made him more intimidating.

He spent over a decade working on luxurious accommodation that he would never live in. Diagnosed with a serious disease, his illness forced him to focus on what really mattered; he knew that, for him, the writing was on the wall. He made a speech about the change in his thinking:

> Remembering that I'll be dead soon is the most important tool I've ever encountered to help me make the big choices in life. Because almost everything—all external expectations, all pride, all fear of embarrassment or failure—these things just fall away in the face of death, leaving only what is truly important.[72]

But he still felt that his own way was the best way, which may have cost him his life. His was a treatable disease, but he chose to ignore the input of his advisors, and may have died prematurely as a result. He chose a vegan diet, herbal remedies, juice fasts, bowel cleansing, and consultations with psychics.

He was worth ten billion dollars when he died on October 5, 2011.

The cofounder of the Apple Corporation, his name was Steve Jobs.

In the two "power encounters" of chapters 4 and 5, we see Daniel confronting two different rulers, in events separated by some sixty years. There are significant differences in the ways in which the two rulers are portrayed. Daniel describes Belshazzar as Nebuchadnezzar's son, but the word may mean "descendant." Some think Belshazzar was Nebuchadnezzar's grandson.

Ernest Lucas writes: "It seems that the writer of the book of Daniel wanted us to compare these two men. The reference to Nebuchadnezzar in verse 2 and then verse 11 prepares the way for an extended comparison between Belshazzar and his 'father.'"[73]

The grace and kindness of God is found here, even in the midst of judgment. Nebuchadnezzar is the most powerful man in the world. He has crushed the nation of Israel, but he responds to grace. In the later years, when God confronts his pride and he responds, he experiences a kind of conversion, a change of heart. At the end of his story, Nebuchadnezzar is presented as the king repentant and restored, mentally, physically, and politically. Those who had acted as his regents during his incapacitation handed the reins of government back to Nebuchadnezzar. Once again, he ruled a glorious kingdom. And he was restored socially. His counselors began to seek him out. God did even more for this king, for "surpassing greatness was added" to him. Grace wins.

What a contrast with Belshazzar, who comes to the throne twenty-three years after the death of Nebuchadnezzar, and is portrayed as stubborn and foolish, and ultimately rejected by God. A corrupt and immoral tyrant, he is presented in this narrative as beyond redemption. The king's decision to use the goblets taken from the Jerusalem temple—kept safe for over sixty years in the treasure house of Babylon—is symbolic of his contempt for Yahweh, and of his own depravity.

Bible commentator Tremper Longman writes of Belshazzar:

Not only is he committing blasphemy, he combines it with idolatry. Here is where his profanation surpasses that of Nebuchadnezzar. He uses God's holy goblets to toast the lifeless idols of his own religion. He spits in God's eye, as it were, and then he goes over to a statue that he himself had created and expects that lifeless hunk to protect him from what was to come.[74]

The vessels were brought to the feast. Belshazzar and his guests drank from them as they praised the gods of the realm. No doubt this praise was directed primarily to the four chief gods of Babylon:

- Marduk, the patron god of the city
- Nebo, god of wisdom, literature, and education
- Nergal, god of war
- Ishtar, goddess of fertility

That very night, Belshazzar the Chaldean king was slain. Apparently, the invaders marched into the banqueting hall and slaughtered the king and his company of merrymakers. The writing, quite literally, was on the wall.

Both kings were guilty of arrogance and pride, but it was Nebuchadnezzar who truly repented of his haughty attitude. Nebuchadnezzar spoke of God's ability to humble the proud. Israel's greatest king, David, knew that truth: "You save the humble but bring low those whose eyes are haughty" (Ps. 18:27).

Humility involves serving, refusing to be boastful, not thinking of ourselves more highly than we ought, but it is also about an attitude of dependence upon the Lord, and knowing that whatever we have or achieve ultimately comes from Him.

It was Nebuchadnezzar's celebration of his own "glory" that triggered his season of humiliation, which led him to true humility.

Again, what a contrast with Belshazzar. Excavation of the ruins of Belshazzar's palace has revealed how much this man revered and celebrated himself. And arrogance was not just seen in the way Belshazzar approaches God. Utterly corrupted by his sense of power, Belshazzar was rude in the way he addressed Daniel, interrogating him as if he were a prisoner, while Nebuchadnezzar spoke respectfully to Daniel.

Another example of the danger of an inflated ego is found in the New Testament. Herod thought too much of himself—and was judged for it.

> On the appointed day Herod, wearing his royal robes, sat on his throne and delivered a public address to the people. They shouted, "This is the voice of a god, not of a man." Immediately, because Herod did not give praise to God, an angel of the Lord struck him down, and he was eaten by worms and died.
>
> But the word of God continued to spread and flourish. (Acts 12:21–24)

God hates pride. Historian Herbert Butterfield wrote: "Judgment in history falls heaviest on those who come to think themselves gods, who fly in the face of Providence and history, who put their trust in man-made systems and worship the work of their own hands, and who say that the strength of their own right arm gave them the victory."[75]

Pride is a virus that often pollutes religion and spirituality. We make more time for prayer, then not only feel superior about our prayerfulness, but soon adopt a superior attitude to those around us, who are apparently not as prayerful.

All of us fail—we've all sinned—but some respond to God's nudges of conviction more readily than others. The writer to the Hebrews exhorts us to maintain tender hearts toward God. God spoke to Nebuchadnezzar three times before He fully got the king's attention, as this commentator states:

> God had spoken once to Nebuchadnezzar in giving
> him the dream of the great image of the times of
> the Gentiles. But the heart of the king was willful,
> and he continued to go on with his own purpose,
> in his pride and folly. God spoke twice by the mar-
> velous vision of the Son of God in the midst of the
> fiery furnace, keeping His faithful witnesses from
> all danger and harm. But again the proud king

kept on his way, with unsubject heart and unsub-
dued will. Now God speaks the third time, and
this in a most humiliating manner, to this great
world-ruler's confusion before his princes.[76]

As Daniel interacts with these two rulers who enjoyed such incredible
earthly power, once again we see the source of ultimate power—
God. And Daniel experiences that power in the place of apparent
powerlessness and weakness: Babylon. Gerard Kelly writes:

> When we were introduced to Daniel in chapter 1,
> it was in the context of a loss of power. On their
> journey from Jerusalem to Babylon, Daniel and
> his friends said goodbye to the freedoms and
> privileges by which they had tended to measure
> the power of their God. They were powerless before
> a world-crushing empire. Daniel in particular is
> subsequently called to stand before a succession of
> Babylonian rulers; he is the pawn facing the king;
> the stateless exile before the focus of all author-
> ity. The very definition of powerlessness stands
> before the personification of power. Like Joseph
> and Moses before him, Daniel has no currency to
> rely on but faith. But it is just in this context that
> he discovers the greatest power of his God. In the

uneven contest of the emperor and the exile, it is the exile—odds on favorite to lose—who carries the day. Through over 70 years in Babylon, Daniel discovers that God's power is rooted in God's faithfulness. He is the source of all power because He is the King of the whole earth—as powerful in Babylon as He ever was in Jerusalem.

And it is also characterized by faithful service, not by pomp and prestige. To the humble exile, captive in a foreign court and stripped of the visible signs of worldly power, God's greatest power is revealed. And it is seen in the long haul of a faithful life. God's power makes it possible to thrive in an alien land. Even without the exile being brought to an end, the superior power of Yahweh is displayed.[77]

How would Belshazzar have been aware of Nebuchadnezzar's humiliation? Certainly the story would have been widely known, but evidence exists that indicates that Belshazzar may have seen these events firsthand.

Belshazzar had probably seen what happened to Nebuchadnezzar, and yet he had still refused to humble himself before the Most High God.

And that made his blasphemy against Israel's God even more inexcusable.

Looking back, I can scarcely
believe what God has done.
I've learned, over the years, that He can be trusted,
that even when all looks lost, He is faithful.
I've learned that when all seems confusing, pray.
That His way is best.
That His blessing will infuriate others.
I've learned to say yes, and no.
And now, I have to stand before yet another king.
One who has never learned.

FOR REFLECTION

1. "Pride is a virus that often infects religion and spirituality." Why is that, and how can we avoid becoming prideful and arrogant?

2. What are the trappings of success?

3. What one lesson of life would you give to your much younger self?

It pleased Darius to appoint 120 satraps to rule throughout the kingdom, with three administrators over them, one of whom was Daniel. The satraps were made accountable to them so that the king might not suffer loss. Now Daniel so distinguished himself among the administrators and the satraps by his exceptional qualities that the king planned to set him over the whole kingdom. At this, the administrators and the satraps tried to find grounds for charges against Daniel in his conduct of government affairs, but they were unable to do so. They could find no corruption in him, because he was trustworthy and neither corrupt nor negligent. Finally these men said, "We will never find any basis for charges against this man Daniel unless it has something to do with the law of his God."

Daniel 6:1–5

In the third year of Cyrus king of Persia, a revelation was given to Daniel (who was called Belteshazzar). Its message was true and it concerned a great war. The understanding of the message came to him in a vision.

At that time I, Daniel, mourned for three weeks. I ate no choice food; no meat or wine touched my lips; and I used no lotions at all until the three weeks were over.

Daniel 10:1–3

A hand touched me and set me trembling on my hands and knees. He said, "Daniel, you who are highly esteemed, consider carefully the words I am about to speak to you, and stand up, for I have now been sent to you." And when he said this to me, I stood up trembling.

Then he continued, "Do not be afraid, Daniel. Since the first day that you set your mind to gain understanding and to humble yourself before your God, your words were heard, and I have come in response to them.

But the prince of the Persian kingdom resisted me twenty-one days. Then Michael, one of the chief princes, came to help me, because I was detained there with the king of Persia. Now I have come to explain to you what will happen to your people in the future, for the vision concerns a time yet to come."

Daniel 10:10–14

I am GOD. I have called you to live right and well.
I have taken responsibility for you, kept you safe.
I have set you among my people to bind them to me,
and provided you as a lighthouse to the nations,
To make a start at bringing people
into the open, into light:
opening blind eyes,
releasing prisoners from dungeons,
emptying the dark prisons.
I am GOD.

Isaiah 42:5–8, The Message

You are the light of the world. A town built on a hill cannot be hidden. Neither do people light a lamp and put it under a bowl. Instead they put it on its stand, and it gives light to everyone in the house. In the same way, let your light shine before others, that they may see your good deeds and glorify your Father in heaven.

Matthew 5:14–16

But you are a chosen people, a royal priesthood, a holy nation, God's special possession, that you may declare the praises of him who called you out of darkness into his wonderful light. Once you were not a people, but now you are the people of God; once you had not received mercy, but now you have received mercy.

1 Peter 2:9–10

The moral life should not be experienced as an agony of impossible choices. It should be a matter of habit and instinct. Learning to live well is about developing the right instincts and habits.

Samuel Wells[78]

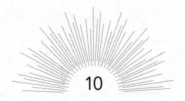

10

Nobody's Looking

It's the part of the airline safety briefing that I've always wondered about, where everyone is informed about rafts and lifejackets being available in the event of a water landing.

Water landing? As far as I know, that short sentence is generally an oxymoron. Planes are designed to set down on land, not water. But once in a great while, somebody comes along and breaks the rules, exceeds the expectations, and delivers what others deem impossible.

Captain Chesley Sullenberger, "Sully," did just that. On Thursday, January 15, 2009, Sully was just one minute into Flight 1549, bound for North Carolina from New York, with 155 passengers and crew on board, when a massive bird strike resulted in the loss of all power in both engines.

A quick response was needed, with the lives of so many in the balance. Sully radioed the ground and considered his next step. Flying back to La Guardia was not an option, no other airports were reachable, so there was only one way forward. The captain informed air traffic control that he would land on the Hudson River.

Such a feat was considered almost impossible, and that Sully managed to land without loss of life or serious injury was seen as a miracle. Sully said that he didn't pray, but rather just reacted as if this were an everyday situation, an incredible testimony to his ability to stay calm under such gargantuan pressure. Later he was to say that he assumed that others were taking care of the praying. Surely, he was right. Steve Chalke wrote:

> After 40 years as a pilot, Sullenberger reacted to the dilemma facing him as if it was second nature. His decision to ditch in the river Hudson wasn't made because the rules told him that was the right thing to do. Neither was he making the decision based on the possible consequences of doing so—after all, planes are not designed to land on water, and most attempts have ended in complete catastrophe.
>
> What allowed Captain Sullenberger to make the decision that turned out to be the "miracle" on the Hudson, was 40 years of experience, training and discipline. Through hundreds and hundreds of flying hours he had developed a set of habits and skills, which though now second nature to him, allowed him to make decisions that were not the obvious choices to make, nor the ones that his pilot's manual would have told him to choose.
>
> Moral success is every bit as much about the formation of good habits, over time, through disciplined effort, as any other skill. And the point of all this training and discipline is that on the day—at the moment of decision—you do the right things naturally.

We have reduced ethics to the moment of decision—the attempt to negotiate hopelessly difficult moral dilemmas—and that is our biggest problem.[79]

While we live in a beautiful world, we know that it is also a world filled with the darkness that sin creates. We all live in Babylon. Darkness leads to hopelessness. John Dominic Crossan writes: "There is no lighthouse keeper. There is no lighthouse. There is no dry land. There are only people living on rafts made from their own imaginations. And there is the sea."[80]

José Martinez, a taxi driver in New York, provides a litany of despair:

> We're here to die, just live and die. I live driving a cab. I do some fishing, take my girl out, pay taxes, do a little reading, and then get ready to drop dead. Life is a big fake. You're rich or you're poor. You're here, you're gone. You're like the wind. After you've gone, other people will come. It's too late to make it better. Everyone's fed up, can't believe in nothing no more. People have no pride. People have no fear! People only care about one thing and that's money. We're gonna destroy ourselves, nothing we can do about it. The only cure for the world's illness is nuclear war— wipe everything out and start over. We've become

like a cornered animal, fighting for survival. Life is
nothing.[81]

So how does God bring people to the light of His love, and restore
hope where there has been hopelessness? He does this through His
people. In Old Testament times, Israel was called to be a "lighthouse
nation," a working, living model of what life lived arm in arm with
God as our senior partner looks like.

Commentator Chris Wright states: "God's answer to the international blight of sin is a new community, a nation that would be
the pattern and model of redemption, as well as the vehicle by which
the blessing of redemption would eventually embrace the rest of
humankind."[82]

Israel was called to be a people—a "kingdom" (Ex. 19:3–6) of
priests, prophets, and politicians that would profoundly affect the
nations of the earth. They would be a prophetic event that provoked
curiosity, and a means of salvation to those who sought it. Their history was written for the sake of the whole of history. As Chris Wright
says, "God called and chose Israel, not at the expense of the rest, but
for the sake of the rest."[83]

We, the church, are now charged with the same role.

In our confused world, God wants a people who live lives that
stand out, models of character and consistency, based on firm foun-
dations. Lloyd C. Douglas, who wrote the novel *The Robe*, tells of a
retired music teacher whom he met while in university. They lived
in the same lodgings, the older man disabled and unable to leave his
apartment. A daily ritual of sorts developed between them; every
morning Douglas would open the old man's door and ask the same
question: "Well, what's the good news?" The older gentleman would

pick up his tuning fork, tap it on the metal arm of his wheelchair, and say the following, which almost has a creedal feel about it:

"That's Middle C! It was Middle C yesterday; it will be Middle C tomorrow; it will be Middle C a thousand years from now. The tenor upstairs sings flat, the piano across the hall is out of tune, but that, my friend, is Middle C!"[84]

We are called to be God's "Middle C" people.

Sixty years have passed since Daniel came to Babylon. He had what one commentator describes as a "remarkable spirit." Previously, we looked at his attitude of excellence. He was utterly consistent: the word used to describe him means "continually distinguished." In short, he was a person of integrity.

The word "integrity" stems from the Latin word *integer*, which means "whole" and "complete." One writer says:

> Integrity requires an inner sense of "wholeness" and consistency of character. When you are in integrity, people should be able to visibly see it through your actions, words, decisions, methods, and outcomes. When you are "whole" and consistent, there is only one you. You bring that same you wherever you are, regardless of the circumstance. You don't leave parts of yourself behind. You don't have a "work you," a "family you," and a "social you." You are YOU all the time.

Given the real definition of integrity, we recognize that it is actually extremely difficult to be in integrity 100% of the time. We aspire to be in integrity with what we believe but sometimes, we mess up. Sometimes, our emotions get the best of us and we are unable to intentionally manage our behavior and actions. Sometimes, we don't give ourselves permission to be our true selves out of fear of what others may think or due to an inability to truly "integrate" the various parts of ourselves into ONE, complete WHOLE person.[85]

Even though life was tough for Daniel, and God surely seemed distant at times, he continued to be faithful. Viv Thomas comments:

Daniel managed to surf the waves of this second choice world and even after all he had been through, he was still skillfully negotiating the white water of Babylon.

Second choice worlds can be worlds of unhelpful or dishonest compromise. Disappointment at not being in our first choice world can cause us to cut corners. I know of one Christian leader who committed adultery because in his mind this was some sort of compensation for not getting a job he wanted. Another stole money from his company because he felt he should have got a promotion and was overlooked. The second choice worlds set up the compromise of integrity and in our weakness we submit. People mostly lose their integrity through a thousand small cuts. They do not take a big decision to head off into a world of pretend and deceit; it happens slowly. The pressure of the second choice world is such that we can start to slide into compromise and only we are aware of it. Somehow Daniel managed to avoid the lingering death of compromise and held on to the core of what it meant to live for God in a hostile second choice world.[86]

Daniel's life was beyond reproach. His political enemies, infuriated by his meteoric rise to dizzy heights of power, and seething with envy, did everything they could to find fault in his life—and they did so in vain. Those running for political office today experience incredible scrutiny—intelligence agencies and the media scan their lives, the latter because they are hungry for scandal to fuel the next lurid headline. How would we do if our tax submissions and expenses claims were similarly scrutinized?

A close look at the members of the 100th U.S. Congress (1987–1989) makes disappointing reading, with 29 being arrested for spousal abuse; 7 convicted of fraud; 19 arrested for writing bad checks; 117 bankrupted two or more businesses; 14 arrested on drug charges; 8 arrested on shoplifting charges; 21 with lawsuits against them; 84 charged with driving while intoxicated.[87]

Being trustworthy means that we can be given power and responsibility, and those who give it to us can be confident we will not misuse what we are stewards of; we will give our best when no human being is watching us.

Daniel was also diligent, and didn't leave important tasks unfinished. It's possible to be busy, yet still lazy, as we keep deferring tasks that we find boring, moving them each day to the bottom of our "to do" lists. In their commentary on Daniel, R. Stortz and R. K. Hughes state, "God just calls us to be reliable, like a family sedan. 'Liable' means to be responsible. 'Re' means over and over again."[88]

Integrity does not just "happen" in our lives.

Character is formed through thousands of everyday choices. Daniel emerges as an extremely intentional, disciplined soul. He is commended because he "set his mind" to gain understanding and humble himself before God. We will look at his prayer life in more detail later, but for now we notice that he set himself to pray three times daily, and also gave himself to seasons of fasting.

Integrity is forged in our character as we walk closely with God each day, and make choices that are good and right. Without integrity, we might attempt a song or two in Babylon, but we will be seriously out of tune.

FOR REFLECTION

1. What do "Middle C" people look like in practice?

2. In what kinds of situations do you find yourself tempted to be a "different you"?

3. Why is disappointment with God potentially a threat to our integrity?

Now when Daniel learned that the decree had been published, he went home to his upstairs room where the windows opened toward Jerusalem. Three times a day he got down on his knees and prayed, giving thanks to his God, just as he had done before. Then these men went as a group and found Daniel praying and asking God for help. So they went to the king and spoke to him about his royal decree: "Did you not publish a decree that during the next thirty days anyone who prays to any god or human being except to you, Your Majesty, would be thrown into the lions' den?" The king answered, "The decree stands—in accordance with the law of the Medes and Persians, which cannot be repealed."

Then they said to the king, "Daniel, who is one of the exiles from Judah, pays no attention to you, Your Majesty, or to the decree you put in writing. He still prays three times a day." When the king heard this, he was greatly distressed; he was determined to rescue Daniel and made every effort until sundown to save him.

Then the men went as a group to King Darius and said to him, "Remember, Your Majesty, that according to the law of the Medes and Persians no decree or edict that the king issues can be changed."

So the king gave the order, and they brought Daniel and threw him into the lions' den. The king said to Daniel, "May your God, whom you serve continually, rescue you!"

A stone was brought and placed over the mouth of the den, and the king sealed it with his own signet ring and with the rings of his nobles, so that Daniel's situation might not be changed. Then the king returned to his palace and spent the night without eating and without any entertainment being brought to him. And he could not sleep.

At the first light of dawn, the king got up and hurried to the lions' den. When he came near the den, he called to Daniel in an anguished voice, "Daniel, servant of the living God, has your God, whom you serve continually, been able to rescue you from the lions?"

Daniel answered, "May the king live forever! My God sent his angel, and he shut the mouths of the lions. They have not hurt me, because I was found innocent in his sight. Nor have I ever done any wrong before you, Your Majesty." The king was overjoyed and gave orders to lift Daniel out of the den. And when Daniel was lifted from the den, no wound was found on him, because he had trusted in his God.

At the king's command, the men who had falsely accused Daniel were brought in and thrown into the lions' den, along with their wives and children. And before they reached the floor of the den, the lions overpowered them and crushed all their bones.

Then King Darius wrote to all the nations and peoples of every language in all the earth:

"May you prosper greatly!

"I issue a decree that in every part of my kingdom people must fear and reverence the God of Daniel.

"For he is the living God
and he endures forever;
his kingdom will not be destroyed,
his dominion will never end.
He rescues and he saves;
he performs signs and wonders
in the heavens and on the earth.
He has rescued Daniel
from the power of the lions."

So Daniel prospered during the reign of Darius and the reign of Cyrus the Persian.

Daniel 6:10–28

Peter and the other apostles replied: "We must obey God rather than human beings!"

Acts 5:29

Yet a time is coming and has now come when the true worshipers will worship the Father in the Spirit and in truth, for they are the kind of worshipers the Father seeks. God is spirit, and his worshipers must worship in the Spirit and in truth.

John 4:23–24

11

Lion King

Daniel and the lions' den: it's certainly one of the most familiar stories of the Bible, a favorite for children. A closer look, however, shows that it is actually an 18-rated (R in America) horror story of political betrayal, conspiracy to murder, and the death of some innocents too, as the wives and children of the conspirators were eaten alive. But the story also points us to the ultimate powerlessness of the most powerful man in the world: Darius, who is trapped by his own legal system, and the supernatural power of God, preserving Daniel in an impossible situation.

This was a trial of "ordeal." Rather than just being a means of execution, it's possible that the lions' den was used to "prove" the integrity or sinfulness of a person. If they survived, they were deemed innocent. Perhaps that's why Darius hurried to the den early in the morning after a restless night. Not only are Christians not promised that we will be spared tragedy, but sometimes having faith makes life more difficult, not less.

Daniel experiences the supernatural protection of God *in* this trial. He doesn't avoid it, but experiences rescue in it. Just as his three friends ended up in the flames, but found there the "fourth man" walking in the fire with them, so Daniel has to spend the night in the pit, but was joined by an angel who protected him.

Gerard Kelly points out the similarities between the two accounts: "In both stories it is the angel of the Lord who comes (3:25; 6:22), in both stories the servants of God emerge totally unharmed (3:27; 6:22) and in both … representatives of paganism are killed instead" (3:22; 6:24).[89]

John Goldingay adds: "As Daniel's friends were not preserved from the furnace, so Daniel has not been preserved from the lion pit; as the divine aide entered the furnace to stand with Daniel's friends, so God has sent His aide into the pit to stand with Daniel; as Daniel's friends were preserved in the furnace, so is Daniel in the lion pit."[90]

Jesus promised His disciples that they would have trouble in this world, but then repeatedly affirmed that they would never be alone, that He would always be with them. That promise is true for us today.

As we saw earlier, this also reminds us that faith should not be dependent upon God bringing about a specific outcome.

Gerard Kelly sums it up: "Faith is not dependent on God's rescue. In both stories those facing death clearly believe that God is able to rescue them—but this is not the basis for their faith. They are loyal to God because He is God, and if they must die for their loyalty, so be it. Faith is rooted in who God is, not in what He does for those who serve Him."[91]

R. Anderson agrees: "The author is not fashioning a doctrine of cause and effect; his purpose is far less speculative and far more practical. Hope does not reside in any human, however powerful, but in God alone. The story of Daniel offers hope, not a remedy. The reader is asked to grasp hold of that hope not as the sure and certain means of deliverance but as an attitude to life."[92]

Darius was the most powerful man on the planet at the time of Daniel, but he was unable to save Daniel. Wonderfully, Daniel had a Helper who had and has far greater power.

According to Walter Wink, Daniel's "seemingly innocuous act" was "more … revolutionary than outright rebellion would have been. Rebellion simply acknowledges the absoluteness and ultimacy of the emperor's power, and attempts to seize it. Prayer denies that ultimacy altogether by acknowledging a higher power."[93]

Daniel's knowledge of God meant that, for him, prayer was his lifeline, and not just a helpline for emergencies. We read that Daniel prayed, "just as he had done before."

At the heart of the entire story of Daniel is the freedom to worship the only true and living God—and an absolute refusal to worship false gods. Whatever else Daniel and his friends were deprived of—family back in Jerusalem, the comforts of home, the familiarity of their own culture—there was one absolute sticking point for them: they would and must worship God (as in Daniel's case here) and they would not bow down to anything other than God.

This vital truth—that worship matters—calls us to be those who worship the Lord freely, gladly, with passion, energy, thoughtfulness, and sacrifice.

We don't know what happened in the lions' den—but we do know what was happening in the palace—Darius was terribly anxious! While Daniel was calm, the king was going through agonies of fear.

It's worth affirming that all claims to the miraculous should be authenticated. Many stories end with "and they all lived happily ever after." Not this one, because when the conspirators and their families were thrown into the lion pit, they were immediately savaged. And the pit itself had been sealed:

"The king sealed it with his own signet: it was common practice to put some clay at the place where the stone met the edge of the entrance to the cave or pit. Then an image would be placed in the fresh clay, using a personal seal. In this case it was the seal of the king himself and those of his noblemen."[94]

Daniel was not spared because the lions were not feeling hungry! The tragic ending of the story authenticates the miracle. God is not glorified by false claims.

Remember that unchangeable edict that Darius had created, one so legally binding that even he could not break it to save Daniel from the lions? Something quite remarkable happens when Daniel emerges from the den unscathed. The king supersedes his own unbreakable edict, and issues a new declaration where he not only declares the supreme greatness of God, but writes to every part of his empire, demanding that they recognize Daniel's God as the true God.

No wonder Scripture declares: "Now to him who is able to do immeasurably more than all we ask or imagine, according to his power that is at work within us, to him be glory in the church and in Christ Jesus throughout all generations, for ever and ever! Amen" (Eph. 3:20–21).

Just as there are strong parallels between the furnace and the lions' den, so scholars see a beautiful consistency between this story and the death and resurrection of Christ. Daniel was sealed into a pit and a stone was rolled over the mouth of the pit to seal it; Jesus went down into the "pit" of death, and was placed in a tomb, and a stone was rolled over it to seal the entrance. No way out—from the furnace, from the lion pit, or from the tomb of death. But when everything has gone wrong, there is still God: Christ was raised triumphant. Daniel was placed in a position of even greater power and honor, and an astonishing statement comes from the mouth of Darius who, perhaps, without knowing it, speaks of the King of Kings to come:

"For he is the living God and he endures forever; his kingdom will not be destroyed, his dominion will never end. He rescues and he saves; he performs signs and wonders in the heavens and on the earth" (Dan. 6:26–27).

Once again, faithfulness changes the world. Many believe that Darius was also known as Cyrus. And it was Cyrus who would issue a later decree releasing the Jews to return to Jerusalem, and rebuild the temple.

> In the first year of Cyrus king of Persia, in order to fulfill the word of the LORD spoken by Jeremiah, the LORD moved the heart of Cyrus king of Persia to make a proclamation throughout his realm and also to put it in writing: This is what Cyrus king of Persia says: "The LORD, the God of heaven, has given me all the kingdoms of the earth and he has appointed me to build a temple for him at Jerusalem in Judah. Any of his people among you may go up, and may the LORD their God be with them." (2 Chron. 36:22–23)

It appears that the man who had witnessed a miracle in a lions' den was the man God used to end the exile. Daniel's influence was nothing short of incredible, world-changing. Without being a ranter or cheesy, Daniel was known as a man of Yahweh. His enemies used his faith against him, because they knew the depth of his godly convictions. In a day when the word "evangelism" seems outdated, we're a people called to live and tell the good news. No loudhailer needed: just us willing it to be known, in public and private, that Jesus is our King.

When they rolled the stone over the entrance, I
thought that this was my last sight of the sky.
I prayed; I hope it won't take long.
Perhaps they won't toy with me, like
cats with a helpless mouse.
If they go for my throat, it will be quick.
The worst would be this: to be eaten alive.
Screaming my way into oblivion.
It goes dark. I hear them, padding around,
their giant paws soft but heavy, their hot breath
coming closer. Which of them is coiled now,
poised to leap, to strike, to end this, to end me?
Seconds, then minutes pass. And it's then
that I sense that presence, thick in the air,
that strong, commanding presence that
I've known before when all seemed lost.
The longest hour of my life ticks by.
And then, incredibly, it is morning,
and I wake. Was it all a dream?
One of them stirs, yawns. And then I know.
God came with me to Babylon.
God came with me into this den of death.
And I hear a voice, a familiar voice, calling
me, ordering the stone to be removed.

For a moment, I wonder. Will the unsealing of
the den unsettle the lions, so that, as I rise to
walk out into the light, they will stir and strike?
I respond to the king. All is well. An angel came.
At last, I emerge, my eyes blinking
against the brightness of the dawn.
The king looks haggard.
He hasn't slept well.

FOR REFLECTION

1. Why do some Christians think that, if we have enough faith, we will be spared suffering?

2. Why is worship so vital and important?

3. Can you think of a situation where you were in a lions' den situation, but God gave you peace in the midst of it?

In the first year of Darius son of Xerxes (a Mede by descent), who was made ruler over the Babylonian kingdom—in the first year of his reign, I, Daniel, understood from the Scriptures, according to the word of the LORD given to Jeremiah the prophet, that the desolation of Jerusalem would last seventy years. So I turned to the Lord God and pleaded with him in prayer and petition, in fasting, and in sackcloth and ashes.

I prayed to the LORD my God and confessed:

"Lord, the great and awesome God, who keeps his covenant of love with those who love him and keep his commandments, we have sinned and done wrong. We have been wicked and have rebelled; we have turned away from your commands and laws. We have not listened to your servants the prophets, who spoke in your name to our kings, our princes and our ancestors, and to all the people of the land.

"Lord, you are righteous, but this day we are covered with shame—the people of Judah and the inhabitants of Jerusalem and all Israel, both near and far, in all the countries where you have scattered us because of our unfaithfulness to you. We and our kings, our princes and our ancestors are covered with shame, LORD, because we have sinned against you. The Lord our God is merciful and forgiving, even though we have rebelled against him; we have not obeyed the LORD our God or kept the laws he gave us through his servants the prophets. All Israel has transgressed your law and turned away, refusing to obey you.

"Therefore the curses and sworn judgments written in the Law of Moses, the servant of God, have been poured out on us, because we have sinned against you. You have fulfilled the words spoken against us and against our rulers by bringing on us great disaster. Under the whole heaven nothing has ever been done like what has been done to

Jerusalem. Just as it is written in the Law of Moses, all this disaster has come on us, yet we have not sought the favor of the LORD our God by turning from our sins and giving attention to your truth. The LORD did not hesitate to bring the disaster on us, for the LORD our God is righteous in everything he does; yet we have not obeyed him.

"Now, Lord our God, who brought your people out of Egypt with a mighty hand and who made for yourself a name that endures to this day, we have sinned, we have done wrong. Lord, in keeping with all your righteous acts, turn away your anger and your wrath from Jerusalem, your city, your holy hill. Our sins and the iniquities of our ancestors have made Jerusalem and your people an object of scorn to all those around us.

Now, our God, hear the prayers and petitions of your servant. For your sake, Lord, look with favor on your desolate sanctuary. Give ear, our God, and hear; open your eyes and see the desolation of the city that bears your Name. We do not make requests of you because we are righteous, but because of your great mercy. Lord, listen! Lord, forgive! Lord, hear and act! For your sake, my God, do not delay, because your city and your people bear your Name."

Daniel 9:1–19

In the third year of Cyrus king of Persia, a revelation was given to Daniel (who was called Belteshazzar). Its message was true and it concerned a great war. The understanding of the message came to him in a vision.

At that time I, Daniel, mourned for three weeks. I ate no choice food; no meat or wine touched my lips; and I used no lotions at all until the three weeks were over.

On the twenty-fourth day of the first month, as I was standing on the bank of the great river, the Tigris, I looked up and there before me was a man dressed in linen, with a belt of fine gold from Uphaz around his waist. His body was like topaz, his face like lightning, his eyes like flaming torches, his arms and legs like the gleam of burnished bronze, and his voice like the sound of a multitude.

I, Daniel, was the only one who saw the vision; those who were with me did not see it, but such terror overwhelmed them that they fled and hid themselves. So I was left alone, gazing at this great vision; I had no strength left, my face turned deathly pale and I was helpless. Then I heard him speaking, and as I listened to him, I fell into a deep sleep, my face to the ground.

A hand touched me and set me trembling on my hands and knees. He said, "Daniel, you who are highly esteemed, consider carefully the words I am about to speak to you, and stand up, for I have now been sent to you." And when he said this to me, I stood up trembling.

Then he continued, "Do not be afraid, Daniel. Since the first day that you set your mind to gain understanding and to humble yourself before your God, your words were heard, and I have come in response to them."

Daniel 10:1–13

I heard, but I did not understand. So I asked, "My lord, what will the outcome of all this be?"

He replied, "Go your way, Daniel, because the words are rolled up and sealed until the time of the end. Many will be purified, made spotless and refined, but the wicked will continue to be wicked. None of the wicked will understand, but those who are wise will understand.

"From the time that the daily sacrifice is abolished and the abomination that causes desolation is set up, there will be 1,290 days. Blessed is the one who waits for and reaches the end of the 1,335 days.

As for you, go your way till the end. You will
rest and then at the end of the days you will
rise to receive your allotted inheritance."
Daniel 12:8–13

In the same way, the Spirit helps us in our weakness.
We do not know what we ought to pray for, but the
Spirit himself intercedes for us through wordless
groans. And he who searches our hearts knows the
mind of the Spirit, because the Spirit intercedes for
God's people in accordance with the will of God.
Romans 8:26–27

If we confess our sins, he is faithful and just and
will forgive us our sins and purify us from all
unrighteousness. If we claim we have not sinned, we
make him out to be a liar and his word is not in us.
1 John 1:9–10

12

Over and Out

Picture an elderly man, his window open, staring out toward the homeland that he has lost. Richard Foster has described prayer as "the heart's true home." It is where we find our peace, the renewal of our identity. As we end our journey through the life of Daniel, we realize that prayer was the conduit through which God empowered him to live with such courage.

Daniel was surrounded by very visible, tangible expressions of power; we've already seen that people could be tossed into furnaces or lions' dens at a king's word. In putting his trust in God during the long haul of his second choice life, Daniel clung to the God he could not see. When we have no *visible* means of support, we must remember that there are limitless resources of *invisible* support.

In 1983, Alexander Solzhenitsyn lamented the loss of God in our culture, and nothing has changed. He wrote:

> The great crisis of humanity today is that it has lost its sense of the invisible. We have become experts in the visible, particularly in the West. If I were called upon to identify briefly the principal trait of the entire 20th century, I would be unable to find

anything more precise and pithy than to repeat
again and again, "Men have forgotten God." The
failings of human consciousness deprived of its
divine dimensions have been a determining factor
in all the major crimes of this last century.[95]

Living in Babylon, and moving in the highest circles of power,
would demand compromises. But Daniel was adamant: just as he
was insistent about worship, he would never deny or abandon his
practice of prayer. Prayer sits at the heart of what it means to be
Christian; we are not just a people who attend religious gatherings,
believe certain biblical ideas, and endeavor to align our lives with
a set of moral and ethical ideals. Rather, we are a people who walk
daily with God in a living relationship with Him through faith.

The prophet Micah put it like this: "He has shown you, O
mortal, what is good. And what does the LORD require of you? To
act justly and to love mercy and to walk humbly with your God"
(Mic. 6:8).

The apostle Paul expressed his all-surpassing ambition with
these words:

I want to know Christ—yes, to know the power of
his resurrection and participation in his sufferings,
becoming like him in his death, and so, somehow,
attaining to the resurrection from the dead.

Not that I have already obtained all this, or
have already arrived at my goal, but I press on to

take hold of that for which Christ Jesus took hold
of me. Brothers and sisters, I do not consider myself
yet to have taken hold of it. But one thing I do:
Forgetting what is behind and straining toward
what is ahead, I press on toward the goal to win the
prize for which God has called me heavenward in
Christ Jesus. (Phil. 3:10–14)

We read that Daniel "turned" to the Lord—this literally means
"I gave God my face." Daniel was determined to look to God in
prayer until the Lord gave him an answer. His prayer was directed
toward "the Lord [adonay] God." The name *'ădōnāy* means "owner,
ruler, or sovereign" and identifies Yahweh as the owner and ruler
of the universe. Not only was He able to hear Daniel's prayer, but
He had the power to direct the affairs of world history in order to
answer that prayer.[96]

And Daniel's prayer was personal, intimate. "Daniel addressed
Yahweh as 'my God'—the basis upon which he was able to approach
the Lord with his requests. He was a child of God. Specifying
Yahweh as 'my God' also emphasizes that Daniel rejected the false
idols of Babylon; his God was Yahweh."[97]

Prayer is far more than an emergency call for help, or the recit-
ing of a wish list; the heart of any relationship is conversation, and
prayer is us naturally, freely, faithfully talking to God. Without
prayer, Christianity descends into a vaguely irritating moral code, a
set of principles that lack purpose. Steve McVey describes the call to
prayer that is surely for us all:

There is an awakening amongst many believers today who are no longer satisfied with the hustle and bustle generally known as the Christian life. Call it the deeper life, the contemplative life, or whatever you will. By any name this quality of Christian life is conceived in divine intimacy and born in quiet moments spent between two lovers. Many Christians who are dissatisfied with the emptiness of the noise are hearing His gentle call to something deeper, richer.[98]

Prayer builds the muscle of faith, and enables us to live courageously. There were plenty of terrifying moments for Daniel and his friends, and probably only some of them are recorded; a fiery furnace and a den of hungry lions to name but two. But there was a fearlessness about these exiles that surely is more than strong character on their part: they experienced supernatural strength. Gerard Kelly writes:

> Perhaps the greatest fruit of a deeper knowledge of God is that we find our fears diminishing. On seventy-nine occasions Scripture records the command, "fear not" and one of the outcomes of deeper prayer in our lives is that when trouble arises, we are less prone to panic. Our response to

pressure is no longer distorted by fear. The opposite of fear, which is not courage but trust, becomes
our foundation. The outworking of this depth and
confidence is seen in the patterns and passions of
Daniel 9. This intercessory prayer projects its trust
in God onto the national and international scene.
The book of Daniel has resources for prayer far
beyond the personal and pietistic; it promotes
a history changing view of prayer's power. We
will have the strength and security, the depth
and discipline to face life's pressures when at the
centre of our being we have learned to draw on
the resources of God's presence. When we know
intimacy with God in the inner sanctuary of the
soul, we will know confidence in God in the outer
battles of our Babylon.[99]

Effective prayer is rooted in a knowledge of God that comes as we
immerse ourselves in Scripture. That was certainly true in Daniel's
prayer life. Gerard Kelly adds:

> Daniel read and understood that Israel's captivity
> in Babylon would last seventy years. He remem-
> bered that he was taken captive in the first wave of
> the captivity, about 606 BC. Seventy years would

bring the end of captivity and would be followed by the restoration of the people to the city of Jerusalem around 536 BC. Jeremiah wrote: "This is what the Lord says: 'When seventy years are completed for Babylon, I will come to you and fulfill my gracious promise to bring you back to this place. For I know the plans I have for you,' declares the Lord, 'plans to prosper you and not to harm you, plans to give you hope and a future. Then you will call upon me and come and pray to me, and I will listen to you. You will seek me and find me when you seek me with all your heart. I will be found by you,' declares the Lord, 'and will bring you back from captivity'" (Jeremiah 29:10–14).

What Daniel read in the Scriptures set him to praying, pleading the promises of God. "You said the desolation would only last seventy years. That is just two years away. Please listen to your servant's prayer, and restore the city and the sanctuary that bear your name." We too need to plead the promises of Scripture.[100]

As we read, reflect upon, and apply Scripture, we fuel our praying. The Bible tells us to confess our sins to God, but Daniel "stood in the gap" for Israel and owned their sins and confessed them to God in prayer.

S. R. Miller comments:

Daniel began to pour out his heart to God as he confessed his sin and the sin of his people Israel. Though he identified himself with his people, Daniel certainly had not been part of the rebellious majority who had brought the wrath of God upon the nation.

Six different aspects of Israel's sin are set forth in vv. 5–6. Israel had "sinned," "done wrong," "been wicked," "rebelled," "turned away" from Yahweh's commands and laws and had "not listened" to Yahweh's prophets. What an indictment![101]

When Cyrus/Darius issued the decree allowing Jews to return to Jerusalem, Daniel didn't join them. Commentators believe that this was probably because he was around ninety years old at the time, so to travel back would have been beyond him. Also, he was still a high-level official in Babylonian government, so he would not have been able to leave his duties. Perhaps he still felt that his calling was to "pray for the prosperity of Babylon," and therefore his calling kept him there.

We don't know exactly how Daniel died, but we do know he lived until a good old age. When he died, he was respected and celebrated in that strange land of Babylon. He was placed in leadership and influence under Nebuchadnezzar, Darius, and possibly Cyrus. Some rabbinic sources suggest that he was killed by

Haman, the wicked prime minister who is the villain of the book of Esther, but we don't know for sure—it's possible that he died of natural causes.

What we do know, as we draw to a close in this book, is that we don't need to fear exile. How do we sing in exile? We need to know that exile in Daniel meant God giving favor, opening doors, granting revelation and insight, helping people take a stroll in a furnace, keeping lions' mouths shut, outliving wicked kings, and being helped when others plot your downfall. In exile, Daniel met angels. He discovered that he was greatly loved by God. And this vital truth is hammered home throughout his story: despite present appearances, God is in control. Heaven rules.

Daniel and his friends tell us that, yes, we too can sing in Babylon.

We can live beautifully as exiles. It's what followers of Jesus have always known. At home, but not at home. Citizens of the nation where we live, but with another, primary identity.

Back in AD 120, a Christian wrote a letter to a distinguished academic, probably the tutor of Marcus Aurelius, the Roman emperor of the day. These words, written back then, have such relevance for us today.

> For Christians are not distinguished from the rest of humanity by country, or by speech, or by dress. For they do not dwell in cities of their own or use a different language or practice a peculiar life. But while they dwell in Greek or barbarian cities, according as each person's lot has been cast,

and follow the customs of the land in clothing and
food and other matters of daily life, yet the condition of citizenship which they exhibit is wonderful
and admittedly strange. They live in countries of
their own but simply as sojourners, they share the
life of citizens, they endure the lot of foreigners.
Every foreign land is to them a homeland and
every homeland a foreign land. They spend their
existence upon the earth but their citizenship is in
heaven.[102]

We read that Daniel was still serving "in the first year of Cyrus'
reign over Babylon." This began in October 539 BC. This would
mean that Daniel's tenure of service extended over a sixty-five-year
period. Through all the twists and turns of life, Daniel was faithful
throughout. As Eugene Peterson said, "Faith is a long obedience in
the same direction."

And faithful, older people can not only be dynamically effective
in their latter years, but bring the fruit of wisdom and experience.

Doug Barnett wrote:

Research into the lives of hundreds of important
people showed that 60 was the average age at which
400 of the famous people of history did their best
work. Many Bible notables were rich in years;

Noah was building an ark when most people of his age are on Zimmer frame instruction. Abraham and Sarah produce children in extremely advanced years. Moses, 80, was leading the people out of the bondage of slavery in Egypt. Caleb, 85, claimed his promised land inheritance after waiting 45 years for it, and was immediately plunged into a fight with his enemies. Joshua, around 70, led the people into Canaan and conflict. Anna, 85, exercised a ministry of prayer in the temple. Paul, 70, declared, "I can do everything through him who gives me strength" in Philippians 4:13. John at 90, composed the book of Revelation.

Their testimony is a clear and simple one—all can serve regardless of age. That service may be different from what has been done before but it need not be less effective … don't regret growing older, it is a privilege that is denied to many people. Rejoice in it and all the potential it holds for you. There are endless number of things that can be done and learned. Never lose your sense of wonder and delight in the possibilities of each day. You can do things in your mature years that couldn't be done when you were younger. What you lack in physical energy you can make up for with spiritual enthusiasm and life commitment. Dare to be a Daniel and stay with the programme until you get promoted to "higher service."[103]

A final word from Gerard Kelly:

The very final bookend in the life of Daniel, given
in the last words of the book, is a remarkable key
to the understanding of a long haul faith. After
the stories of trial and triumph; after the long life
of faithful service; after the dreams and visions of
the future in which the sovereign God wins all,
Daniel is told by an angel quite simply to get on
with his life.

Eugene Peterson's translation of the Bible para-
phrases the angel's words:

"And you? Go about your business without
fretting or worrying. Relax. When it's all over you
will be on your feet to receive your reward" (Dan
12:13 *The Message*).

The promise is of a future kingdom—a future
resurrection. There is an inheritance to come, but
the immediate call is to perseverance and faith. An
old man, perhaps tired of waiting for the fulfill-
ment of the dreams his God has given him, Daniel
is sent, in effect, back into exile. It is in the here and
now reality of Babylon that he must press onto the
very end. Deliverance is promised, but the promise
is not yet delivered.

There is a day coming when exile and alienation, trauma and trial will be no more. But that
is the "not yet" of God's kingdom. The "now" is a

world waiting for the touch of God's grace; a world
deep in thrall to false gods; deep in the darkness of
injustice. The now is Babylon. The power of God is
given for your exile.[104]

Sometimes I forget that, in Jesus, I am going to live forever. I don't
lose my faith, I just mislay it. Because we determine that faith is not
pie-in-the-sky, we forget the glorious future. Grief accelerates that
amnesia. When I held a box of ash in my hands, the last remains
of the man I used to call Dad, the possibility of a future reunion to
come seemed remote. Death seeks to have the last laugh, sneering at
the resurrection hope that is ours. But Daniel ends his words to us
with a reminder that he would take his place in the communion of
saints: forever.

And let's remember that Daniel was not *just* promised life
forever: and neither are we. Our resurrection hope does not center
around just beating death and experiencing endless life in the luxu-
ries of heaven. Rather it's all about us being with God, and Him
being with us, in close company, up close and personal, for always.
Let's jump back to one of Daniel's dreams, where he saw Jesus.

As I looked,

thrones were set in place,
and the Ancient of Day took his seat.
His clothing was as white as snow;
the hair of his head was white like wool.
His throne was flaming with fire,

and its wheels were all ablaze.
A river of fire was flowing,
coming out from before him.
Thousands upon thousands attended him;
ten thousand times ten thousand stood before him.
The court was seated,
and the books were opened. (Dan. 7:9–10)

And again:

In my vision at night I looked, and there before
me was one like a son of man, coming with the
clouds of heaven. He approached the Ancient of
Days and was led into his presence. He was given
authority, glory and sovereign power; all nations
and peoples of every language worshiped him. His
dominion is an everlasting dominion that will not
pass away, and his kingdom is one that will never
be destroyed. (Dan 7:13–14)

Jesus repeatedly referred to Himself as the Son of Man (Matt.
12:8, 32, 40; Matt. 16:13, 27, 28; Matt. 17:9; 19:28; Mark 2:10;
8:31). The expression "the Son of Man" occurs eighty-one times in
the Greek text of the four canonical gospels, and is used only in the
sayings of Jesus.

We turn to the book of Acts, and witness Stephen dying an
agonizing martyr's death. As they pummel his body with stones, he
has a vision:

But Stephen, full of the Holy Spirit, looked up to heaven and saw the glory of God, and Jesus standing at the right hand of God. "Look," he said, "I see heaven open and the Son of Man standing at the right hand of God." (Acts 7:55–56)

In the book of Revelation, the white-haired Son of Man appears again in power and glory:

I turned around to see the voice that was speaking to me. And when I turned I saw seven golden lampstands, and among the lampstands was someone like a son of man, dressed in a robe reaching down to his feet and with a golden sash around his chest. The hair on his head was white like wool, as white as snow, and his eyes were like blazing fire. His feet were like bronze glowing in a furnace, and his voice was like the sound of rushing waters. In his right hand he held seven stars, and coming out of his mouth was a sharp, double-edged sword. His face was like the sun shining in all its brilliance.

When I saw him, I fell at his feet as though dead. Then he placed his right hand on me and said: "Do not be afraid. I am the First and the Last. I am the Living One; I was dead, and now look, I am alive for ever and ever! And I hold the keys of death and Hades." (Rev. 1:12–18)

In exile, our future is certain. We shall be with Jesus, be like Jesus, and with Him always. The exile from the old Jerusalem over, the joy of His presence in the new Jerusalem ours.

Joni Eareckson Tada writes:

> In C. S. Lewis's *Last Battle*, the concluding book in the Chronicles of Narnia, there was not the usual "and they lived happily ever after." Instead, on the last page of this book, after scores of exhilarating adventures and journeys in all the previous books, C. S. Lewis wrote that now he had come to the beginning of the real story. All the previous chapters of adventures in Narnia had only been the cover and the title page. The real Chapter One was about to begin, a story no one on earth had ever read, which would go on forever and ever with each chapter better than the last.[105]

Together with one another, together with God: we really can be a beautiful, melodious choir, singing the kingdom song, one that celebrates Jesus, King of Kings, Lord of Lords.

And He shall reign.

Forever.

Hallelujah.

FOR REFLECTION

1. Why is prayer difficult?

2. How do you pray most effectively?

3. What strategies might you adopt to ensure faithfulness to God until the end?

4. What does it mean to live in the light of eternity?

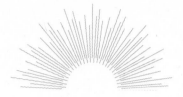

Notes

1. Viv Thomas, *Second Choice: Embracing Life as It Is* (London: Formation, 2018).

2. Gerard Kelly, *Sing the Lord's Song in a Strange Land: Spring Harvest Study Guide* (Uckfield, UK: Spring Harvest, 2005).

3. Larry Osbourne, *Thriving in Babylon: Why Hope, Humility, and Wisdom Matter in a Godless Culture* (Colorado Springs: David C Cook, 2015), 10.

4. Gerard Kelly, *Sing the Lord's Song in a Strange Land: Spring Harvest Study Guide* (Uckfield, UK: Spring Harvest, 2005).

5. John Lennox, *Against the Flow: The Inspiration of Daniel in an Age of Relativism* (Oxford: Monarch, 2015), 14.

6. Gerard Kelly, *Sing the Lord's Song in a Strange Land: Spring Harvest Study Guide* (Uckfield, UK: Spring Harvest, 2005).

7. Gerard Kelly, *Sing the Lord's Song in a Strange Land: Spring Harvest Study Guide* (Uckfield, UK: Spring Harvest, 2005).

8. Viv Thomas, *Second Choice: Embracing Life as It Is* (London: Formation, 2018).

9. Donald McCullough, *The Consolations of Imperfection* (Ada, MO: Brazos Press, 2004).

10. Tremper Longman III, *The NIV Application Commentary, Daniel,* (Grand Rapids, MI: Zondervan, 1999).

11. brainyquote.com/quotes/leo_tolstoy_105644.

12. Tom Wright, *Acts for Everyone* (London: Society for the Promotion of Christian Knowledge, 2010).

13. J.R.R. Tolkien, *Lord of the Rings: The Fellowship of the Ring* (London: Allen & Unwin, 1966), 60.

14. Debra Veal, *Rowing Alone* (London: Robson Books Ltd, 2003).

15. Paul Steinberg: *Speak You Also: A Survivor's Reckoning* (New York: Henry Holt, 2000), 47.

16. Book of Jasher 44:76.

17. businessinsider.com/beautiful-people-make-more-money-2014.

18. journals.plos.org/plosone/article?id=10.1371/journal.pone.0025656.

19. J. G. Baldwin, *Daniel* (Vol. 23, p. 89) (Downers Grove, IL: InterVarsity Press, 1976).

20. Tremper Longman III, *Daniel, NIV Application Commentary* (Grand Rapids, MI: Zondervan, 1999), 50.

21. R. K. Harrison, *Israel's Apostasy and Restoration, Essays in Honor of R.K. Harrison,* Avraham Gileadi, ed. (Grand Rapids, MI: Baker, 1988).

22. Gerard Kelly, *Sing the Lord's Song in a Strange Land: Spring Harvest Study Guide* (Uckfield, UK: Spring Harvest, 2005).

23. Erwin Raphael McManus, *Wide Awake: The Future Is Waiting within You* (Nashville: Thomas Nelson, 2012).

24. studyinternational.com/news/schools-21st-century-skills/.

25. Jonathan Edwards, *The Works of Jonathan Edwards*, ed. Perry Miller, vol. 13, *The Miscellanies*, ed. Thomas A. Schafer (New Haven, CT: Yale University Press, 1994), 483.

26. loc.gov/collections/alexander-graham-bell-papers/articles-and-essays/inventor-and-scientist/.

27. Michael Frost, *Seeing God in the Ordinary: A Theology of the Everyday* (Peabody, MA: Hendrickson, 2000).

28. hewlett.org/listening-with-empathy/.

29. The story is told in Tim Harford's excellent book, *Adapt: Why Success Always Starts with Failure* (London: Abacus, 2011).

30. John Bright, *Israel and the Nations*, republished as *A History of Israel.*

31. E. H. Peterson, *The Message: The Bible in Contemporary Language* (Colorado Springs: NavPress, 2005).

32. R. Stortz and R. K. Hughes, *Daniel: The Triumph of God's Kingdom* (Wheaton IL: Crossway Books, 2004), 18.

33. Walter Brueggemann, *Hopeful Imagination: Prophetic Voices from Exile* (Minneapolis: Fortress, 1986).

34. John Lennox, *Against the Flow: The Inspiration of Daniel in an Age of Relativism* (Oxford: Monarch 2015), 47.

35. Michael Griffiths, *Cinderella with Amnesia* (London: IVP, 1975), 7.

36. John Goldingay, *Daniel* (Dallas: Word, 1989), 24.

37. Tremper Longman, *Daniel: The NIV Application Commentary.*

38. Jeff Lucas, *Grace Choices* (Milton Keynes: Authentic Media/Spring Harvest, 2004).

39. James Freeman, *The Customs, Etiquette and Traditions of the Old Testament* (Morrisville: Lulu Press Inc., 2013).

40. Gerard Kelly, *Sing the Lord's Song in a Strange Land: Spring Harvest Study Guide* (Uckfield, UK: Spring Harvest, 2005).

41. Walter Brueggemann, *Hopeful Imagination: Prophetic Voices from Exile* (Minneapolis: Fortress 1986).

42. Gerard Kelly, *Sing the Lord's Song in a Strange Land: Spring Harvest Study Guide* (Uckfield, UK: Spring Harvest, 2005).

43. Tremper Longman, *Daniel: The NIV Application Commentary* (Grand Rapids, MI: Zondervan, 1999).

44. Richard Patterson, "Faithful to the End," Bible.org.

45. churchtimes.co.uk/articles/2019/27-september/news/uk/corbyn-hails-invaluable -work-of-churches.

46. Viv Thomas, *Second Choice: Embracing Life as It Is* (London: Formation, 2018).

47. churchtimes.co.uk/articles/2005/18-november/books-arts/book-reviews/what -has-christianity-ever-done-for-us-its-role-in-shaping-the-world-today.

48. goskybound.com/10-tips-to-leading-volunteers.

49. Stanley Hauerwas and William H. Willimon, *Resident Aliens: Life in the Christian Colony.*

50. Elie Wiesel: *All Rivers Run to the Sea: Memoirs, Vol. One 1928–1969.*

51. Karestan Koenen, professor of psychiatric epidemiology at the Harvard T.H. Chan School of Public Health, nationalgeographic.co.uk/history-and-civilisation /2020/03/panic-spreading-coronavirus-heres-why-we-evolved-feel-anxiety.

52. Dallas Willard, *The Divine Conspiracy* (London: Harper Collins, 1998), 71.

53. Dallas Willard, *The Divine Conspiracy* (London: Harper Collins, 1998).

54. edition.cnn.com/2008/WORLD/africa/06/24/mandela.quotes/.

55. Yann Martell, *The Life of Pi*, quoted in topologymagazine.org/quote/only-fear -can-defeat-life/.

56. Dietrich Bonhoeffer, *Life Together* (London: SCM Press, 1995).

57. Graham Tomlin, *The Provocative Church* (London: Society for Promoting Christian Knowledge, 2014).

58. Gerard Kelly, *Sing the Lord's Song in a Strange Land: Spring Harvest Study Guide* (Uckfield, UK: Spring Harvest, 2005).

59. David Smith, *Mission after Christendom* (London: Darton, Longman and Todd, 2003).

60. Eugene Peterson, *The Message: The Bible in Contemporary Language* (Colorado Springs: NavPress, 2005).

61. Viv Thomas, *Second Choice: Embracing Life as It Is* (London: Formation, 2018).

62. Pete Greig, *God on Mute* (Ada, MO: Baker, 2011).

63. John Lennox, *Against the Flow: The Inspiration of Daniel in an Age of Relativism* (Oxford: Monarch, 2015), 152.

64. Viv Thomas, *Second Choice: Embracing Life as It Is* (London: Formation, 2018).

65. Philip Yancey, *Where Is God When It Hurts?* (Grand Rapids, MI: Zondervan, 2002).

66. Philip Yancey, *Where Is God When It Hurts?* (Grand Rapids, MI: Zondervan, 2002).

67. Dr. Gordon Temple, Torch Trust for the Blind.

68. Richard Wurmbrand, *Tortured for Christ*, independently published, 1967.

69. Anna Lee Stangl, from the Preface of *Tried by Fire* (London: Monarch, 2003).

70. Apology 50, Tertullian, quoted in Gerard Kelly, *Sing the Lord's Song in a Strange Land: Spring Harvest Study Guide* (Uckfield, UK: Spring Harvest, 2005).

71. Taken from *Spoken Worship: Living Words for Personal and Public Prayer* by Gerard Kelly Copyright © 2007 by Gerard Kelly. Used by permission of Zondervan. www.zondervan.com.

72. azquotes.com/author/7449-Steve_Jobs.

73. Ernest Lucas, *Apollo OT Commentary* (Nottingham, UK: IVP Academic, 2002).

74. Tremper Longman III, *Daniel: The NIV Application Commentary* (Grand Rapids, MI: Zondervan, 1999).

75. Herbert Butterfield, *Christianity and History* (New York: Scribner, 1950).

76. H. A. Ironside, *Lectures on Daniel the Prophet* (New York: Loizeaux Bros, 1953), 59–60.

77. Gerard Kelly, *Sing the Lord's Song in a Strange Land: Spring Harvest Study Guide* (Uckfield, UK: Spring Harvest, 2005).

78. Samuel Wells, *Improvisation: The Drama of Christian Ethics*, 75.

79. Steve Chalke, *Different Eyes: Spring Harvest Study Guide* (Uckfield, UK: Spring Harvest, 2009).

80. John Dominic Crossman, *The Dark Interval* (Salem, OR: Polebridge Press 1994).

81. David Friend, *The Meaning of Life* (Boston, Little Brown, 1991).

82. Chris Wright, *Living as the People of God*, (London: IVP, 1983).

83. Chris Wright, *Living as the People of God*, (London: IVP, 1983).

84. This famous story is variously quoted, including in Donald McCullough's *The Trivialization of God: The Dangerous Illusion of a Manageable Deity* (Colorado Springs: NavPress, 1995), 66.

85. huffpost.com/entry/the-true-meaning-of-integ.

86. Viv Thomas, *Second Choice: Embracing Life as It Is* (London: Formation, 2018).

87. R. Stortz & R. K. Hughes, *Daniel: The Triumph of God's Kingdom* (Wheaton, IL: Crossway Books, 2004) 91.

88. R. Stortz & R. K. Hughes, *Daniel: The Triumph of God's Kingdom* (Wheaton, IL: Crossway Books, 2004).

89. Gerard Kelly, *Sing the Lord's Song in a Strange Land: Spring Harvest Study Guide* (Uckfield, UK: Spring Harvest, 2005).

90. John Goldingay, *Daniel* (Dallas: Word, 1989).

91. Gerard Kelly, *Sing the Lord's Song in a Strange Land: Spring Harvest Study Guide* (Uckfield, UK: Spring Harvest, 2005).

92. R. A. Anderson, *Signs and Wonders: A Commentary on the Book of Daniel* (Grand Rapids, MI: Wm. B. Eerdmans Pub. Co., 1984).

93. John Goldingay, *Daniel* (Dallas: Word, 1989).

94. R. Péter-Contesse and J. Ellington, *A Handbook on the Book of Daniel* (New York: United Bible Societies, 1993), 169.

95. Alexander Solzhenitsyn, during his speech on receiving the 1983 Templeton Prize.

96. Adapted from John Goldingay, *Daniel* (Dallas: Word, 1989).

97. S. R. Miller, *Daniel* (Nashville: Broadman & Holman Publishers, 1994), 242.

98. Steve McVey, *The Divine Invitation* (Eugene, OR: Harvest House, 2002).

99. Gerard Kelly, *Sing the Lord's Song in a Strange Land: Spring Harvest Study Guide* (Uckfield, UK: Spring Harvest, 2005).

100. Gerard Kelly, *Sing the Lord's Song in a Strange Land: Spring Harvest Study Guide* (Uckfield, UK: Spring Harvest, 2005).

101. S. R. Miller, *Daniel* (Nashville: Broadman & Holman, 1994).

102. Epistle of Mathetes to Diognetus, newadvent.org/fathers/0101.htm.

103. Doug Barnett, quoted in Gerard Kelly, *Sing the Lord's Song in a Strange Land: Spring Harvest Study Guide* (Uckfield, UK: Spring Harvest, 2005).

104. Gerard Kelly, *Sing the Lord's Song in a Strange Land: Spring Harvest Study Guide* (Uckfield, UK: Spring Harvest, 2005).

105. Joni Eareckson Tada, *Heaven: Your Real Home* (Grand Rapids, MI: Zondervan, 1995), 63.